The Mystery Teachings in World Religions

Throughout the centuries man has searched for that which he could call God, Truth, Law, or some other name that represented ultimate Reality. Various great teachers have come in different ages and to different peoples and have proclaimed transcendental truths which have later developed into the religions of the world. But because of man's tendency to entomb all living truth in rigid and unchanging systems, these religions have often become separative and sometimes even antagonistic.

Florice Tanner's book shows that man's basic truth—which is the way to full self-consciousness at every level of his being—lies hidden in every world faith, whatever the superficial differences may be. She writes from deep personal conviction and in a lively, readable manner. Long accustomed to presenting ideas clearly and creatively, she has conducted summer teacher training courses in six universities in the United States and Canada, and has done special guidance work with gifted children. Presently she maintains a Retreat and Meditation Center in the Great Smoky Mountains in Virginia.

THE MYSTERY TEACHINGS IN WORLD RELIGIONS

By

FLORICE TANNER

A QUEST BOOK ORIGINAL

Published under a grant from the Kern Foundation

THE THEOSOPHICAL PUBLISHING HOUSE
Wheaton, Illinois, U.S.A.
Madras, India London, England

The Theosophical Publishing House, Wheaton, Illinois,
is a department of The Theosophical Society in America

Manufactured in the United States of America

Tanner, Florice.
The mystery teachings in world religions.

(A Quest book original)
Includes bibliographical references.
1. Religions. I. Title.
BL80.2.T29 291 73-8887
ISBN 0-8356-0439-X

ACKNOWLEDGMENTS

My thanks are due to Manly Hall for permission to quote from *The Secret Teachings of All Ages, Twelve World Teachers, The Noble Eightfold Path,* and *Journeys in Truth*; to the Vedanta Center to quote from Swami Paramanda's translation of the *Upanishad* IV-V-VI pp. 28-29; to the Theosophical Publishing House in Madras, India to quote from Annie Besant's *Four Great Religions, Seven Great Religions,* and the translation of the *Bhagavad Gita*; and for permission to quote from *The American Theosophist* in an article by Howard Murphet, p. 126, Spring 1967. Also, I express gratitude to Dorothy Elam, Mary Jane Newcomb, Helen Zahara and Diane Burckes for invaluable help in editing, and to all others who have aided.

"MANKIND COMES TO ME ALONG MANY ROADS, AND ON WHATEVER ROAD A MAN APPROCHES ME, ON THAT DO I WELCOME HIM, FOR ALL ROADS ARE MINE." The Bhagavad–Gita

CONTENTS

FOREWORD

THE PLAN

The great aim and purpose of man, the thinker, in evolution is to reach self-consciousness at all levels of his being. Through sensitizing and transforming his present physical and mental equipment, he strives, step by step, toward self-mastery and attainment of the highest powers. Each man faces the challenge of directing his personal vision toward mankind's highest hopes in order to reach the potentialities that will ever expand as he grows toward his own spiritual maturity.

The plans for universal structure have been given; the correlation between things has been clarified; and the keys to the accumulated wisdom of the ages are available. Consciousness of the Absolute goes beyond the limits of all the various force fields which scientists explore. A nonmaterial Reality transcends the transitory fields in which man usually thinks and lives. This larger awareness of Reality is the potential within man. The energy which is expressed in cyclic processes is precipitated from this potential.

The operation of these cyclic processes in evolution is unfolding the potential Reality at various levels of consciousness in orderly sequence. Everything is conscious at its own level and on its own plane of perception. Man's challenge is to become self-conscious, not only at his present physical level, but also at each level of development. Knowledge and instruction to this end have been handed down and are available. A man may choose to evolve slowly with the masses or he may quicken his evolution.

Many ways to express a great universal plan have been used in the East. One of the clearest and most inclusive describes a ladder of consciousness which extends from the simplest forms in rocks, plants, animals, and formative nature energies, to the highly developed "Adepts" and superhuman men. The Hindu belief recognizes that all forms of consciousness are in a continual process of change and growth. Even the great "Adepts" and "Masters" are still evolving toward higher grades of consciousness.

The Eastern seers recognize that the evolution of consciousness and form is a very slow process, and therefore they record developments in vast eras of time. Only in the last hundred or so years have the Western scientists verified time calculations in billions instead of thousands of years.

The ancient teaching is that a great plan lies behind all this vast process of slow change. Cycles of growth and visible change alternate with periods of rest which also include change. The process continues, cycle after cycle. This pattern of change is a continuum in all life forms and in consciousness as well. Scientists call this process of changing forms "evolution." The Eastern scholars call the process of changing consciousness "reincarnation." At the human level each man makes choices that increase or retard his progress, but at best the process is exceedingly slow.

Growth in consciousness has been aided through the ages by man's longing to be part of a greater whole. Universal concepts of oneness have extended man's thoughts and aspirations. Religions have fostered his yearning to belong and his devotion to higher hopes. Great leaders have guided the people so that man has attained ever widening understanding. Each civilization, with its beliefs and understandings, has influenced those which followed. Nevertheless, each contributed its unique emphasis. Gradually beliefs stressed by the original teachers were modified. As centuries passed, many variations or sects branched out from the original teachings, and their countless customs and ceremonies made it most confusing for anyone trying to find the deeper meanings. Forms, rather than the significant understandings, were often emphasized.

We need to search out the essentials of every religion, to seek its real values. Especially we need to search for those basic truths which are common to each of them. Behind the ceremony and symbols, behind the various forms of ritual, there are deep truths. No attempt should be made to persuade people to adopt one or another religion. There is no need for division or argument because the differences are usually concerned only with form, the outer showy part. Various outer forms appeal to people of different temperaments. The more emotional prefer one type, those more intellectual choose another. Much of the essence in spiritual values is identical in each of the great religions, of course, because they stem from the same Source. We need to study the similar teachings that are spiritual in nature and universal in scope.

The religions of the future, like those of the past, will be built upon the values which preceding religions have found helpful. They too will be built upon our needs and be adjusted to our stage of development. History records how learned teachers have appeared at critical times to help the people develop definite ideas and skills they needed. Such teachers did not travel far from their own territory. They seldom wrote books, but their influence spread, first to a few, then to great numbers. The particular emphasis they taught was later built into succeeding religions and cultures and became world-wide in influence.

One is filled with wonder and appreciation for the greatness of this unfolding plan, a plan clear and definite in structure. Five unique phases have marked man's development, each of which extended over vast time spans.

The fifth major stage of evolution might be subdivided into a number of different types but they have many similar basic characteristics. Some of these are the Indian type, the Egyptian-Arabian cultures, the Iranian-Persian, the Greek-Roman-Celtic, and the Anglo-Saxon-Teutonic types. Present day peoples represent a most complex intermingling of all forms and levels of consciousness.

A culture developed in India so ancient that oral traditions and only much later records, such as epic poems and myths, form much of our source of information. These traditions indicated that great leaders would guide humanity as they developed characteristics suitable for a culture and succeeding cultures. Changes would come to pass as different combinations of the earlier groups intermarried and formed new types. During vast epochs these groups would migrate as they intermingled and developed.

The early people of India were taught great respect for doing one's duty, both to one's fellow men and to the one Divine Life. A second development came in the people who grew up in Arabia, Egypt, and Africa. Here the teachers stressed the same ancient truths of the One Life in every man but emphasized light and wisdom as the symbol of God. A third section, from west central Asia and Persia, stressed purity. Their leaders used fire as the symbol of God. Later still a fourth type developed in the territories we know as Greece and Rome. These people too were taught similar concepts. Although their leaders had different names and used different forms and ceremonies, they gave to the evolving people according to their needs. Great emphasis was placed upon perfection of form. Beauty and law have come to us from the Greeks, Romans, and Celtic peoples. The Teutonic peoples formed a fifth classification. The teachings of the Christ emphasized individual self-sacrifice and compassion.

In order to truly study this great evolutionary plan,

we must search for the truth. We cannot be bound by any one point of view that our culture, our parents, or other authorities have taught. We must be willing to look at many new and old ideas. We must then honestly judge what seems reasonable and constructive. We are not agreed on any one particular philosophy. We are searching for the fundamental, universal principles of all philosophies and religions. From these we may hope to satisfy our needs and aspirations. We worship truth, not a personality or individual teacher.

If the theory is true that the development of consciousness, both in the race and in the individual, is a continuum, it matters little whether we call it evolution, the law of cause and effect, reincarnation, or some other name. The important concept to realize is that apparently law and order have influenced development during the past ages. The choice of words used to describe this plan should not confuse the concept of ordered progression. Presumably in the future the same law and order will unfold new insights.

It is so easy to become confused if one looks at the strange figures of speech used or the strange customs and rituals that have been established over a long period of time. It is difficult to realize that nations or groups of people have different needs because of their different psychology and nature. The understandings and customs as started by a great leader were definite and clear when given, but over several hundreds of years men have added to them or formed new groups with modified practices. We see how this has happened in the Christian religion and other modern religions. Sometimes these changes are so complex that even religious leaders forget what the original symbols and rituals meant. It is easy to see only the outer forms. This is the reason the beliefs of others are often misjudged. If we would surmount this confusion we need to search for those values common to all the great religions.

The common heritage gives us a few broad doctrines. Almost every religion, for instance, teaches the One Life or the unity of God. Often repeated through the ages is the thought that the one God is known in three ways. Philosophers describe three qualities such as power or will, love-wisdom, and active intelligence. Religions often personify these aspects as three kinds of characters. Repeatedly God is thought of as one in nature but triple in manifestation.

Most religions outline graded spiritual intelligences, with archangels, angels, shining ones, or formative nature energies, called by different names but all "sons of God." Man is at his own place, according to his development, on this evolutionary ladder. He too is a spiritual intelligence and a son of God. Many religions teach that consciousness develops toward more perfection; that there are cyclic changes both on earth and in unseen dimensions; that a law and order characterize nature and the outer world as well as inner development; and that great teachers appear to inspire people and guide evolution.

The age of separatism, where each person feels himself apart from others, is truly passing. We are learning to recognize the common ideals which unfold as we grow. The contribution emphasized by each great religion, as it develops, enriches all of us. The perception of unity in great variety broadens us. As we recognize common values, the plan of universal brotherhood, indeed, comes nearer and we begin to sense our own place in its realization.

Chapter 1

UNITY OF GOD

A vast period of time was needed to develop earliest man's form and simple consciousness, but even more vast were the preceding eras necessary to develop earlier life forms. Small changes may have taken millions of years. Scientists, with the carbon 14 test and tree-ring calibrations, are calculating time more nearly as do occult searchers, in much greater time spans. But at least we know that the span from mineral or vegetative existence, where there is little awareness, to individualized consciousness represents almost unimaginable time.

Through the ageless wisdom, handed down to us from many lands and from different centuries, we find evidence that man has long had knowledge of a oneness of being. Usually, though, man is not consciously aware of this basic unity. He often feels separate and alone. Our civilization is in a transitional stage between one in which the individual feels separate, and one in which he feels himself to be an individualized unit of a universal whole. As man develops he realizes his own oneness with the "unifying ground" in all life. This unity may gradually become a conscious awareness relating all consciousness and form.

Hindu Concepts of Unity

Hinduism or Brahmanism had its roots in prehistoric times but became known in India, according to some historians about 3200 B.C., according to others at a much earlier date. The spiritual truths were handed down orally for centuries and much later were incorporated in their sacred writings, the *Vedas.* The wisdom of the *Vedas* is thought to have been given by initiate teachers at the dawn of man's development to guide the people. The spiritual truths of the *Vedas* are completely implied but not fully described. They are the principal source of esoteric teachings. The foundation for all faiths was given in them. Each of the later world religions was built on this early foundation. Each became a different emphasis of the one vast concept.

The *Upanishads* are an important part of the *Vedas,* giving the mystical and philosophical teachings. As the people evolved they learned better to understand this great system, based upon the invisible world's expressing by evolution toward a more perfect whole. There are as many forms of ritual and organization in Hinduism as there are in other religions. Sacredness is the essence of religion and does not depend upon religious organization.[1]

Other early writings give the lesser knowledge which codifies the sixty-four sciences of nature and the methods of gaining knowledge. Later writings include the *Puranas,* a vast collection of songs, stories and poems embodying Hindu sacred teachings in popular form for the people; the great heroic epics, the *Ramayana* and the *Mahabharata,* still greatly loved in India; and expressions in drama, such as the *Kalidasa.* All these have been given to train the people gradually to understand the hidden spiritual truths. In addition, there are the writings called the Dharmasastras, systematic treatises concerning the conduct of life, and the sutras, which cover the six major systems of Hinduism, upon which innumerable commentaries have been written.

The *Mahabharata,* one of the great epic poems of India, centers around the feud between two ancient clans which probably lived some fifteen centuries before Christ. The *Bhagavad-Gita* is the best known part of this great Hindu poem. The *Gita,* sometimes called "The Lord's Song," was given by Shri Krishna to his disciple, Arjuna. It has brought comfort and strength to many troubled hearts facing the battles of daily life. In the historic poem the struggles between two families symbolize the struggles of the spirit against the lower passions of the physical body and teach that the "I" is involved in a great evolutionary plan. The Self, or truth seeker, must give up all affections for kindred, for possessions, for aspirations, and for worldly ambitions. This is a tremendous battle of loyalties.

Arjuna struggles to know his duty when he sees his own kinfolk among the enemy. Shri Krishna advises him to fulfill his duty and serve the greater good without selfishness or fear. Sacrifice, the giving of all for the common good, is the one deed which brings no blame. The purposes of the Changeless One cannot be defeated or destroyed. The Eternal Being fills all the universe and every creature. Life is imperishable and "birth" and "death" are illusions. The motive which impels an action is the real test.

The *Bhagavad-Gita* teaches that the spiritual man lives in calm, continual contemplation and in union with Divine Life, even while his physical body and mind are active in daily duties. A man can bring his life into harmony with divine law by subduing all selfish energies. The little self becomes one with the higher Self and is not affected by desires or aversions, pleasure or pain. Moderation or an equilibrium between all pairs of opposites is life's goal. Shri Krishna shows that the essence is in the mental attitude rather than in the physical act. The poem teaches the pupil not to be

> . . . attracted by the attractive, nor repelled by the repellant, but [he] must see both as manifestations of the one Lord, so that they may be lessons for his guidance, not fetters for his bondage.[2]

The pupil is instructed to do his duty impersonally as life's responsibilities and position impose, realizing that the great law is working out an evolutionary plan. If the fighting is done without passion or desire but performed as duty, the self is free, giving peace.

The story is symbolic of the soul's struggle in which Shri Krishna, the Logos, gives guidance to Arjuna. The pupil is taught to aspire to his own highest Self. Through the higher Self alone can he understand the nature of the force acting through him and thereby succeed in merging with the light of the Logos.

The concept of the unity of all forms of life with the one unseen Source is found throughout Hindu literature. The Hindu seers realized that absolute reality is the total potential. Multiplicity is transcended in the mystical experience and an awareness of truth, so a nonduality is realized. The Eastern teacher would identify the individual Self with the Universal Self. This dissolving of the center of self-interest (the separate "I" or "me"), this abandonment of the sensory self, is sought in striving to attain "Samadhi." The Buddhist likewise, although not speculating about the ultimate "Ground of the Universe," seeks a similar state called "Nirvana." The great teachers instilled this basic, all-inclusive idea during the first stages of development, and it has continued as each of the succeeding cultures and forms of religion has evolved. Each religion has uniquely expressed the concept; each has emphasized, predominantly, one particular characteristic. The Hindu culture emphasizes man's duty to the one God and to all forms of consciousness in which God manifests. Some quotations from Hindu literature express unity in this way:

> In the highest golden sheath is spotless, partless Brahman, That, the true light of lights, known to the knowers of the Self.[3]
>
> When He is manifest, all is manifested after Him; by His manifestation this all becomes manifest.[4]
>
> When there is no darkness, neither day nor night, neither being nor nonbeing, there is Shiva even alone. He is indestructible. He is to be adored by

Savitri, from Him alone comes forth the ancient wisdom. Not above, nor below, nor in the midst can He be comprehended, nor is there any similitude for Him Whose name is infinite glory. Not by the sight is established His form; none beholds Him by the eye. Those who know Him by the heart and the mind, dwelling in the heart become immortal.[5]

That One (the Absolute), though motionless, is swifter than the mind. The senses can never overtake It, for It ever goes before. Though immovable, It travels faster than those who run. By It the all-pervading air sustains all living beings.

It moves and It moves not. It is far and also It is near. It is within and also It is without all this.

He who sees all beings in the Self and the Self in all beings, he never turns away from It (the Self).[6]

Buddhist Concepts of Unity

Gautama Buddha spent forty-five years, after his illumination, teaching the Hindu people in India. He had been reared in the Hindu traditions which had been evolved many thousands of years before his birth in 623 B.C. Gautama spoke to the people with the religious background familiar to them, often referring to their ancient scriptures in his discussions. He gave teachings in a less metaphysical and more practical form and applied the purest Hindu morality to daily living. His work in India served to reinforce the purity of the earlier teachings.

Many Brahmins were his disciples. He often criticized others, even the monks in his order who were deceived by outward appearances instead of developing purity within. He spoke clearly and directly of current abuses. His message was an attempt to reform corruption by emphasizing individual responsibility of right action, for bringing about great causal changes.

Buddha did not speak of God, the one Source, but he shared with his countrymen the Hindu background and the knowledge of the changeless law out of which changing diversity comes. The Buddhists emphasize the immutable law in the universe which they can prove, rather than speaking of "God" as the source of all unknown causes. Their philosophers and scientists study causes and effects. They recognize that an infinite, omnipresent being cannot be limited by anything outside himself. The "One Life" penetrates, and is the essence of, every atom. For man, apart from himself, there is no God. A universal life is in the microcosm and in the macrocosm with no external creator. Buddhists do not speak of a personal or impersonal God but rather of boundless eternal matter, its energy and motion. They study matter in its visible form and in its many invisible gradations. Nature, the great whole, draws from herself; outside of it nothing can exist.

Gautama's teaching was based on the theory that ignorance caused the world's miseries. To dispel the ignorance, he guided man to develop latent possibilities leading him to self-knowledge and awareness of his personal relation to the universe. The great ones to whom Buddhists aspire are human beings who raised themselves above the ignorance of the race by right action and right thought. They are god-men who learned to live intelligently with true spirituality.

Becoming an individual means entering an existence in which one feels separated temporarily from the one life. Many lifetimes are needed to gain mastery. In later development man will learn to merge his individual self again with the source, and at such time sorrow and ignorance will cease. Thus life is a continuing process of development in which a man's present existence is only a small segment of unfolding. After many lives in the world, a man's consciousness will again be reabsorbed into the larger life process. The highest attainment for man is a state of consciousness in which the past, present, and future blend into the eternal now. It is called "Nirvana."

Attachment to physical existence prevents a man from sensing his unity with life. Buddha realized that the ignorant would continue with their attachments and desires, putting possessions above wisdom and personalities above principles. Thus they would continue to travel the slower path of evolution. The wiser ones might make faster progress by self-knowledge and self-mastery if they would give up one possession after another. Eventually then such souls might attain all.

Perfect peace and tranquility are the symbol of Buddha's attainment. The various statues of the Buddha scattered throughout the world emphasize these two characteristics. Although he was surrounded by many things he remained ever conscious of eternity and the permanence of spirit.

Buddha taught his disciples to live humble, unassuming lives, showing kindness toward all. Each form of life owes its being to others, so he taught that each should serve others. Separateness is considered ignorance, and oneness is wisdom. Buddha said:

> He who is not happy with nothing will not be happy with everything; he who does not cherish the little things will not be thoughtful of the great things; he with whom sufficient is not enough is without virtue, for the physical body of man lives only from day to day; if you supply it with what it actually needs, you will still have time to meditate, while if you seek to supply it with all it wants the task is without end.[7]

The essential teachings of Gautama Buddha are contained in three divisions of literature. The rules for the monastic order and some of the more mystical teachings for training the monks are contained in the *Vinaya.* These books for the advanced pupils speak of the invisible worlds. The second division, the *Sutras,* give Buddha's ethical teachings, discussions, questioning, and explanations in the common language (now called *Pali*). The

Sutras or *Suttas* are given to the common people and concern daily life. The third division is called the *Abhidhamma* and contains philosophical and mystical writings.

Early Buddhism in India was established by monks whose practices of meditation, self-imposed poverty, and abstract rules had little appeal to the common people. Some leaders felt that Buddhism would never help the masses unless changes were made. Two main schools of thought developed. One branch, which moved southward to Ceylon (Sii Lanka), continued the austere practices and was called the Theravada or Hinayana School. It taught that none but those who renounced the world could hope to attain Nirvana.

The other branch, which moved eastward and northward toward China and Tibet, was vitalized by several outstanding leaders. Its scriptures carried full accounts of the invisible worlds and of perfected beings, and the secret teachings which Buddha entrusted to some of his disciples.

During Gautama's day individual development was emphasized. But gradually the Northern Mahayana School gave larger merit to initiate-teachers who consecrated their wisdom and service to human betterment, rejecting the bliss of Nirvana until all of mankind received illumination. These teachers were called "Bodhisattvas." The invisible hierarchy of the many Buddhas, Bodhisattvas, and Arhats is recognized as coming to aid men. The use of ritual, devotion and magical practices increased. Gautama, at first revered as the perfectly enlightened teacher, later was worshiped.

An average person could learn to control his thoughts and emotions and assume responsibility for his actions. The initiate went beyond these responsibilities. By right action, personal refinement and enlightenment, his consciousness could develop toward a godlike state. Beyond this is the Eternal One. Esoteric religion emphasizes the absorption of self into this Universal Oneness.

The monk's strong interpretation of Gautama's teachings so effectively reformed the structure of Brahmanism that the Hindu people were antagonized and the monks finally had to flee from India. The formal center of Buddhism shifted eastward during the third and fourth centuries. By the sixth century the patriarch Bodhidharma left India and permanently established the Mahayana School in China. He brought with him the teachings later known as the Japanese Zen System. It taught the practice of meditation in which all sentient phenomena were considered unreal.[8] Zen emphasizes a universal philosophy in which good works alone earn the privilege of enlightenment. Self-discipline and enlightened action, regardless of sect or creed, bring the individual to the ultimate attainment. Because of the danger of misconception in the use of words, the Zen Buddhist transmitted esoteric traditions for more than a thousand years without words spoken or written. The Zen disciple receives instruction, as have others, through intuition to attain "Satori."

Chinese Concepts of Unity

A great ethical system spread in China until its teachings influenced more than one fourth of the world's population. Confucius, also known as the "Master K'ung," was born in Lu about 551 B.C. He was one of the world's great philosophers who brought hope to his people as his maxims and wisdom influenced their lives.

His informal questioning method, filled with humor and great breadth, emphasized five relationships: "Jen" or goodness, the ideal relationship between human beings; "Chun-tzu," manhood at its best; "Li" or the highest ideal in social life (ceremonials); "Ti" or the power which rules man by virtue; "Wen" or the art of peace. His social concerns stressed moral order and the way of personal conduct.

The harmony of past ages in China had been established by each person identifying himself with tribal traditions, but in the transitional period in which Confucius taught he recognized that men had become more individualized, reflective, and more self-conscious. He encouraged retaining the traditions of old China which had spontaneously sustained order, but he added a deliberate tradition sustaining social ethics. Correct attitudes toward collective well-being were emphasized in every way possible until such habits became the way of life.

The Chou dynasty had brought in the idea of "T'ien" or Heaven, the one power which ruled society, and later Confucius referred to the "Way of Heaven" as sanctioning his whole process of education to produce a Way (Tao) expressing virtue and harmony. He avoided lesser phenomena such as omens and strange experiences but sought to reform religion through ethics. For instance, he discouraged human sacrifice, a practice that had been common before his time.

Side by side with Confucius and his realistic social concerns was another teacher, Mo-tzu, who taught that social reform should come to China not by force but by love. This theory, known as "Mohism," taught 500 years before Christ that the warring factions could be brought to peace only by brotherly good will and kindness toward all. Such equal affection seemed to Confucius too sentimental and impractical; instead he proposed answering "hatred with justice."

Different writers express opinions differently because often original writings are in cryptic style and not presented in a continuous theme. The Master Lao-tzu (604 B.C.) is usually credited with expressing Taoism in *Tao Te Ching,* although there is evidence that a number of "Old Masters" may have contributed to the writings. Actually little is known of Lao-tzu.

The Tao was frequently used by Confucius to mean "a way of life" which he recommended and which was sanctioned by Heaven. Lao-tzu's Tao means more. It stands for an inexpressible source of being. It is a principle which is basic in the world, a divine plan which underlies nature. It is referred to as the mother of all, the passive female principle in contrast to the active male factor. Basic to early Taoism is the idea that true results are attained through inaction or passivity. Nature is effortlessly active although inactive.[9]

Man's purpose is to attain harmony with the Tao through awareness of the beauties and peacefulness in nature. Man is to become self-sufficient and is not to rely upon wealth, prestige, or artificial social life. The wise man is taught to quiet his senses and appetites, to gain an inner perception of the Tao, to achieve harmony with the oneness of the eternal principle which underlies the whole world, and to gain intuitive enlightenment.

Basic attunement with the universe, *wu wei,* is "life lived above tension."[10] The Supreme action takes place below the level of awareness when freedom flows through the person as conscious effort yields to a power beyond the personality. Being is followed by action: "The way to do . . . is to be." One who identifies life with the Tao lets "The Way" work through him. The simplicity and naturalness of the Taoist is quite the opposite to the rigid formalism developed by followers of Confucius. A man whose life is grounded in the Tao lets life flow in and out without abruptness or tenseness, in strong, supple selflessness.

The unity of Taoism is expressed in the ancient Chinese symbol of polarity as *yang* and *yin.* It is pictured as a circle in which the opposite tensions of life are not flatly opposed but rather complement and counterbalance each other. Each invades the territory of the other and establishes a center there, then turns and interchanges place. This constant interchange is a phase of a revolving wheel, since life bends back upon itself and finally knows that "at center all things are one." This symbol of *yang* and *yin* pictures the Taoist attitude toward relative values, avoidance of all clean-cut dichotomies and absolutes. Even birth and death are but related phases in the continuum of life.[11] Expressions of unity in Taoist teachings read:

> He who would gain a knowledge of the nature and attributes of the nameless, undefinable God (Tao) must first set himself free from all earthly desires.[12]
>
> Man takes his law from the earth; the earth takes its law from heaven; heaven takes its law from the Tao.[13]
>
> By words the Tao may not be expressed; What can be thus expressed is not the Tao.[14]

Shintoism

Merging here and there with Buddhism is the early Shinto religion of Japan. Shinto means the "Way of the Gods." The Japanese people go to their temples for private meditation. There is no holy book, creed, or sacrament, but they address their respect to the "kami" which is a superior Being indicating the life force in nature. The Japanese temperament has great affinity to nature and beauty, and as time has passed, Shintoism has often merged with the Buddhist religious practices.

Jainism

Jainism developed in India along with Buddhism under the leadership of Mahavira, who was born about 600 B.C. Preceding him had been a number of Jinas or "Victorious Ones" who had attained Nirvana. Their purpose has been to reform Hinduism although they were usually conservative and unaggressive. They emphasize purity of living and refrain from taking life. They believe in harmlessness, since all life is one, and they strive toward attaining Nirvana. An expression of Jainism says:

> That which is One in Many, Many in One, yet neither One nor Many—I bow to That.[15]

Sikhism

At a much later time, Sikhism (like Buddhism and Jainism) became a movement to reform the formalism in Hindu ceremony and to rid it of hatred and sham. Forced by circumstances, the followers of Sikhism became a militant group, and the Sikh is now often thought of as a daring warrior. The movement, developed in the midst of Hindu culture, is basically devotional.

Ten gurus or teachers followed the first Sikh, Guru Nanak (1469-1539). They organized religious communities, gathered Sikh scriptures, and worked to bring together the warring faiths of Islam and Hinduism. Gradually they were forced, in self defense, to organize as a body separate from both Hinduism and Islam. Finally the tenth Guru, both as a religious and militant leader, raised the Sikh's empire in the Punjab. The group was relatively small and after a few years was overwhelmed by the Muslim empire of the north; still later the land passed to the British. Devotion to the One God, to the multiplicity within the unity is ever emphasized by the Sikhs, along with the attempt to purify life and to withdraw from sham and formalism. A hymn used by the Sikhs reads:

> There is one God,
> Eternal Truth is His Name.
> Maker of all things
> Fearing nothing and at enmity with nothing,
> Timeless is his image;
> Not begotten, being of his own Being;
> By the grace of our Guru made known to man.

The universal quality of nature is expressed in scriptures of Sikhism:

> He Himself is One, and He Himself is many
> He does not die or perish.
> He never comes or goes.[16]

Ancient Hermetic Concepts of Unity

The burning of the Serapeum under the edict of Theodosius, The Good, was a sad deed of vandalism by the early Christian Church Fathers. About 400,000 parchment scrolls were destroyed, and the accumulated wisdom of 10,000 years was lost. Only fragments remained, carved in stone and incised in clay tablets, and most of those which have been recovered were found in tombs.

In 1799, the Rosetta Stone was discovered with its hieroglyphs and many rows of Greek letters. Napoleon placed it in the Cairo Institut National and had copies of the stone distributed to the learned of Europe. This stone furnished the key from which Egyptologists have translated the fragments left by the great Egyptian civilization. But the main problem has been to understand the meanings beneath the familiar words which they translated. For this inner meaning, the scholars had no key.

According to ancient tradition there lived in Egypt a teacher, Hermes Trismegistus, who was called "The Thrice Greatest": the greatest of all philosophers, the greatest of all priests, the greatest of all kings. He was credited with establishing writing, art, history, mathematics, medicine, law, religion, astronomy, chemistry, astrology, divination, architecture, and chronology. He made laws, determined the rights of people, taught how land and property should be divided, worked out a system of measurements and weights, and modified the calendar.[17]

This great teacher, known by many names—"Thoth," "Tahuti," "Theuth" in Egypt—and in the West called "Hermes," was the personification of wisdom, the initiator who had an inexhaustible supply of knowledge recorded in approximately 20,000 books. Some scholars think he was a mythological personage credited with works that actually accumulated during many centuries, as the tribes intermingled in Northern Arabia and Africa.

His work might be a composite result of several leaders. He may have been a mortal who was deified at some remote time because of his benefits to the people. At any rate, he was messenger of the recognized One Light and Wisdom in all.

Gradually through the mingling of tribes and culture the Egyptians developed a central teaching which emphasized light, long before the Christian Bible was written. The Great Troth first said the familiar words [the] "Light which lighteth every man that cometh into the world." His transcendent learning taught the ruler to "Look for the Light," for only as he saw the divine light in his people could he truly rule, and they could be worthy only as they were "following the Light." He taught the people to recognize the light in the heavens and the light within man, animals, vegetables, and minerals, and to find God, the Light, in all.

These people, living on the borders of the Mediterranean, used human energies to influence the subtler worlds. "Magic" or the finding of the correspondences between man, the microcosm, and the mighty macrocosm in which they lived gave them surpassing knowledge. Wise men traveled from all parts of the world to learn the wisdom of Egypt which Hermes Trismegistus had taught.

The Egyptian Messiah was not a personage coming at a specific time. Rather, the ancients watched the rhythmic appearance of planets and stars and in their constant repetitions found assurance of an unfailing fulfillment. For them there was no such thing as "to be saved" for all eternity. "Becoming" took place in the life of man and in nature at all times. "Becoming" was a process expressed in a symphony of relationships; each step, each cycle, each rhythmic pulse of life, fulfilled each creature's being by carrying it onward. Egyptian "magic" included the knowledge and use of these rhythmic pulsations in man and nature. The Egyptians attained great skill in using what we might call "different frequencies of consciousness" in the plant and animal kingdoms as well as in themselves.

Hermetic books now known are probably recent versions of earlier writings. The seventeen fragments of the *Divine Pymander* seem to have been known only since the second century. It is an allegorical account of philosophical and mystical truths. Its deeper meanings are frequently not comprehended. Hermes preached:

> O people of the earth, men born and made of the elements, but with the spirit of the Divine Man within you, rise from your sleep of ignorance! Be sober and thoughtful. Realize that your home is not the earth but in the Light! Why have you delivered yourselves over to death, having power to partake of immortality? Repent, and change your minds. Depart from the dark light and forsake corruption forever. Prepare yourselves to climb through the Seven Rings to blend your souls with the eternal Light.[18]

The Book of Thoth reveals sacred processes by which the regeneration of humanity can be accomplished. Its pages are covered with hieroglyphic symbols which give, to those who are instructed, power over spirits of the air and the subterranean divinities. It also gives the key to other mysteries and has been faithfully preserved through the ages by initiates. Many other fragments, both in stone and on papyrus, give us meager knowledge of the light and wisdom of ancient Arabia and Egypt. The Spiritual Sun, whose essence was invisible, was their Formless One. The visible sun, giving life to form, was their symbol of a universal father.

During many thousands of years, the convictions of the tribes and clans in western Asia and Africa were interchanged. One of the early Egyptologists, de Rouge, described the religion of the people of the Nile Valley as "pure monotheism manifesting itself externally by symbolic polytheism." The conviction of One God continued. The tribes of Arabia, Africa, West Asia, and the Mediterranean territories taught the people in various ways of the One Source of all. From these intermingling peoples has come the foundation for many modern beliefs. Hermetic teachings became reflected in the Jewish concepts, later in the Christian and Muslim concepts, and still later in modified beliefs of other groups. Each stage of development is influenced by concepts inherited from preceding cultures.

Some Egyptian Hermetic expressions of unity state:

Holy is God, the Father of all things, the One who is before the First Beginning.
Holy is God, whose will is performed and accomplished by His own Powers which He hath given birth to out of Himself.
Holy is God, who has determined that He shall be known, and who is known by His own to whom He reveals Himself.
Holy art Thou, who by Thy Word (Reason) hast established all things.
Holy art Thou, of whom all Nature is the image.
Holy art Thou, whom the inferior nature has not formed.
Holy art Thou, who art stronger than all powers.
Holy art Thou, who art greater than all excellency.
Holy art Thou, who art better than all praise.
Accept these reasonable sacrifices from a pure soul and a heart stretched out unto Thee.
O Thou Unspeakable, Unutterable, to be praised with silence!
I beseech Thee to look mercifully upon me, that I may not err from the knowledge of Thee and that I may enlighten those that are in ignorance, my brothers and Thy sons.
Therefore I believe Thee and bear witness unto Thee, and depart in peace and in trustfulness into Thy Light and Life.
Blessed art Thou, O Father! The man Thou hast fashioned would be sanctified with Thee as

Thou hast given him power to sanctify others with Thy Word and Thy Truth.[19]
I Thy God am the Light and the Mind which were before substance was divided from Spirit and darkness from Light.[20]

Zoroastrian Concepts of Unity

Zoroastrians think of the first principle of cause as the "Boundless Circle of Unknown Time," or the Ageless One, also called "Zeroana Akerne." Out of this radiant one emerged all the objectified manifestations. Like the Hindu and Egyptian religions, this great religion expresses the One Creative Radiance. The Zoroastrian doctrine symbolizes this unity as fire. Man is taught to seek within himself the source of this cleansing light; the fire within purifies and burns all that is not truth. When truth is established the great work of perfecting man is accomplished.

The teacher of this faith, Zarathushtra (or in Greek, Zoroaster) taught the disciplining of the mind, making it pure so that eventually it could become cosmic intelligence ("Vohu Manah"). Man has the ability to transcend the finite intellect and reach deep levels in supramental awareness. By meditation he seeks intuitively the relationship of the Divine Spirit within and without. Man's inner Self, the Cosmic Fire of the Spirit, ever burns with the light of intelligence and with the emotions of pure love, but man must actualize these potentials in his living. Life is an instrument for cultivating spiritual relationships.

From the One Existence, unknowable by human faculties, came forth Ahura Mazda, the first created. He is described as the source and the fountain of the life of man. He holds a position similar to that of Brahma of the Hindu scriptures. Ahura Mazda is the invisible pure spirit, the ever-present, eternal and all-pervading reality.

Zarathushtra taught his pupils to recognize this reality

and to seek harmony with it. Great emphasis was put on fire as a symbolic, purifying agent. Man was taught to live in purity that he might devote his thoughts and acts to Ahura Mazda.

The *Avesta* is the principal religious book with its Zends or commentaries on the teachings of Zarathushtra. The interpretations are derived from an ancient sacred language known as "Senzar." This language of signs, of symbols, of colors, of sounds, forms a secret code of certain words known only to initiates. It is said to have been verified and learned in modern times, even as it was learned and used thousands of years ago. Sanskrit and the Avestaic language have the same archaic root; in it occult instructions are given without use of clumsy articulated physical tongue-language. Dr. W. Gray Walter has stated that there is a tendency to "an entirely holistic view of brain function . . . events in the brain are not a single sequence in time."[21] Our present language patterns may indeed be much more clumsy than Senzar communications.

When Alexander burned the huge library of Persepolis, only fragments of Zoroastrian literature remained; later they were taken to Greece where at least parts of them were preserved. The *Yasna* are five fragments of which the archaic hymns or *Gathas* give the prophet's teachings; the second part contains prayers and ceremonies. The *Visparad* is a collection of invocations; the *Nasks* deal with the sciences; the *Venidad* is a book of laws about purity; the *Khordah Avesta* are prayers for the common worship. The *Desatir* is another book containing occult truths. These fragments of a great teaching remain, but they give only a glimpse of the Zoroastrian dignity and original beauty. Here are some Zoroastrian expressions of unity:

> Ahura Mazda (Asura Mazda) himself issued from Zeroana Akerna, "Boundless (circle of) Time," or the unknown cause. The glory of the latter is too

> exalted, its light too resplendent for either human intellect or mortal eye to grasp and see. Its primal emanation is eternal light, which, from having been previously concealed in Darkness, was called to manifest itself, and thus was formed Ormazd, the "King of Life." He is the "first born" in Boundless Time, but like his own antetype (pre-existing spiritual idea) has lived within Darkness from all eternity.[22]

> I am the Protector, I am the Creator, I am the Nourisher, I am the Knowing, I am the Holiest Heavenly One, My name is Healing. . . . My name is God, My name is Great, Wise One; My name is the Pure . . . . I am called the Watcher . . . . The Augmenter, (etc., listing seventy-two names).[23]

> He (Ahura Mazda) first created, through His inborn luster, the multitude of celestial bodies, and through His intellect the good creatures, governed by the inborn mind Thou, Ahura Mazda, the Spirit who are everlasting, makest them (the good creatures) grow. When my eyes behold thee, the Essence of Truth, the Creator of life, who manifests His life in His works, then I know Thee to be the primeval Spirit, Thou Mazda, so high in mind as to create the world, and the father of the good mind.[24]

Other Concepts of Unity

In the west central part of Asia, a number of other religious sects gradually formed, for it was here that the caravans crossed between East and West exchanging goods, ideas, and philosophies. The "Near East" usually means two large cultural groups: the Christian Balkan States and the Asiatic countries of the Arab States, Syria, Lebanon, Israel, Iraq (Persia), and Asiatic Turkey. The Arab States are dominated by the Islamic faith with the exception of Israel, which has Jewish, Muslim, and Christian communities, and Persia, in which Zoroastrian influence still exists.

The intermingling of the peoples and cultures in these lands has been reflected in their music, art, literature, and human convictions, but the mergings make it difficult now to classify their various faiths. The Islamic faith influenced vast numbers of people. The Arabian prophet Mohammed, born about 570 A.D. in Mecca, taught that Allah was the monotheistic God. Islam means "bowing to" or "surrendering to" the will of God. Mohammed said, "All men of whatever faith who surrender themselves to the will of God are truly children of Islam." The teachings revealed to Mohammed were recorded in the *Koran* (Al Quran). He attempted to raise the level of his countrymen above cruel idolatry, licentiousness, and murderous wars to a devotion to God, the One Ruler.

From the eighth to the fourteenth centuries, the Muslims carried learning wherever they conquered. They established the University of Cairo in Egypt, of Bagdad in Arabia, of Cordova in Spain. They taught the forgotten sciences of astronomy, botany, chemistry, mathematics, and scientific agriculture. They developed new types of architecture and music. They translated ancient books of philosophy and brought inventing and manufacturing to a high level of excellence. During the Dark Ages in Europe the followers of the prophet Mohammed maintained the highest civilization in the world. Spain was an example of enlightenment and civilization for nearly eight centuries. From there Muslim influence caused science, literature, art, and philosophy to spread throughout France, England, and Germany.

The orthodox Muslims were limited by their literal beliefs whereas those gifted with larger understanding and deeper vision recognized the spiritual integrity of each enlightened faith, since all religions had the same broad objectives and the same methods for extending consciousness and attaining internal security. Originally Mohammed had taught the tolerant view that all prophets of whatever faith came from Allah to aid the people, and that each, by surrendering his will to God, represented the faith of Islam.

Unity is expressed by the Islamic faith in the following:

> To Allah (God) belongeth the east and the west; therefore, whithersoever ye turn yourselves to pray, there is the face of Allah; For Allah is omnipresent and omniscent.[25]

> Say God is one God. He begetteth not, neither is He begotten; and there is not anyone like unto Him.[26]

After the death of Mohammed in 632 A.D., civil wars broke out and ambitious tyrants catered to the privileged classes, departing from the simple teachings of their prophet. To counteract the corruption of their time, the early Sufis developed austere practices of a mystical nature. They held steadfastly to the spirit of Mohammed's revelation, detaching their minds and emotions from involvement in luxuries and worldly concerns and directing their consciousness toward understanding divine love and tranquillity.

The Sufis also developed a symbolic language and composed songs and poems that were apparently sensual and amorous but that served to hide their real concepts. As the Islam faith drifted further from the original teaching of Mohammed, the position of the Sufis became more hazardous. Although entirely free from Muslim orthodoxy, the Sufis had to disguise their enlarged and deepened concepts in song and poems. The "beloved" in their songs was Truth, not a woman. Divine Wisdom, the "Virgin of the World," was their unattainable mistress.[27] Their "cup of wine" was the power of God giving an ecstasy to the wine of life. Westerners know best the poems by Omar Khayyam but there are said to be five hundred thousand Sufi writings in the Cairo libraries alone. Union with divine reality was covered in their poems by apparent fatalism and a complete detachment from materialism.

Modern Sufis' trends are away from all formalism, toward simple devotional practices which develop internal peace. Sufism reveals an admirable quality of devotion to God and service to man. Recent Sufis have been guided by Meher Baba who has a large following in the United States and hundreds of thousands in various parts of the world. He has reiterated the need to actualize purity, devotion, love, and oneness.

The Sufis express unity thus:

> Thou art absolute Being; all else is but a phantasm,
> For in Thy Universe all beings are one.
> Thy world-captivating Beauty, in order to display its perfections,
> Appears in thousands of mirrors, but it is one.
> Although Thy Beauty accompanies the beautiful,
> In truth the unique and incomparable Heart-enslaver is one.[28]

> O Thou that hast no place in any place — art appearing . . . in every place within this wheeling world, yet cannot be encompassed by my eyes.[29]

The Druses of Syria and neighboring areas were influenced by the beliefs of the many religious faiths in that area. The average Druse members believed they could unite religions and erase fanatical tendencies. The Druse doctrine of tolerance toward each group seemed to be resented by both Muslim and Christian groups. For self-protection the Druses conformed publicly to orthodox practices but privately they dissented and concealed their membership. They are a sect which arose about the eleventh century in the Muslim faith but have been strongly influenced by Gnostic ideas, even as Mohammed was influenced by Christian ideas.

Although made up of intense, militant tribes and clans, the modern Druseans usually share the mystical attitudes of the Sufis and Dervishes. They believe the physical body, with its mental and emotional attributes, hinders the spiritual purposes of man which unites him with the all-pervading universal Spirit. The Druse system impersonalizes and enlarges spiritual convictions. It envisions the religions of the world as becoming aware of unity. Druse teachers guide mankind, and their ceremonies of initiation are designed to change or alter the disciple's condition of consciousness. The influence of their teaching spread as the medieval crusaders returned to Europe. Although the Druseans were a small group they contributed to overthrowing physical and intellectual feudalism, thus helping to bring about the Renaissance and Reformation.

The twelve principal Dervish orders are also a mystical sect which developed in western Asia. Members are initiated by rites which seem fantastic. There are two main types of members: first, the consecrated scholars who study the spiritual forces in the universe, and second, the religious beggars. There is also said to be a secret advanced brotherhood which might have members even among the most lowly beggars. The brotherhood of directors or "Lords of Souls" are said to have renounced everything concerned with physical life and devote their lives to perfecting consciousness. Rising above sense perception and the intellect, they transcend usual understanding and become absorbed into the nature of Universal Being.

The members give allegiance to a governing chief called the "Axis" or "Pole" of the universe, and a series of "Master Souls" form a hierarchy under him. They possess power and wisdom superior to ordinary men and constitute an invisible government which controls the temporal institutions of Islam.

Dervish mystics do not depend upon any orthodox allegiance but each one survives upon his own efforts. He is dedicated to charitable work, internal peace, and depends upon direct extrasensory experience for his guidance. Some Dervishes develop prophetic insight and other remarkable proficiencies. Some abuse powers and spread misunderstandings. The more advanced orders contribute to the knowledge of mysticism, meditation disciplines, and the esoteric possibilities of advancing latent human capacities.

The Baha'i faith began in the last century in the Kingdom of Iran (Persia) and spread throughout the world. Its prophet was Baha'ullah who lived from 1863 to 1892. It is one of the recent attempts to recognize the teachings of many prophets who teach similar great truths, who believe in one God although named differently. Baha'is teach that vision should be world-embracing and not confined to the individual, and that man should dedicate himself to serving the human race.

These concepts of unity are referred to in their writings:

> That which the Lord hath ordained as the sovereign remedy and mightiest instrument for the healing of all the world is the union of its people in one universal Cause, one Common Faith.
>
> Each individual is following the faith of his ancestors who themselves are lost in the maze of tradition. Reality is steeped in dogmas and doctrines. If each investigates for himself, he will find that Reality is one; does not admit of multiplicity; is not divisible. All will find the same foundation and all will be at peace.

Orphic and Platonic Concepts of Unity

The tribes and cultures which pushed westward across Asia and Asia Minor into Europe were vigorous and became great tradesmen and held the Mediterranean coast and seaports for many centuries, long before the Greeks we know in history. Other tribes moved from Asia Minor into Europe settling in Albania, others slowly moved into Italy, France, Belgium, the British Isles, Switzerland, Germany, and even a few into Scandinavia. They were not usually tall in stature but had brown hair and eyes and round heads. They were imaginative, artistic, enthusiastic, and were called "Celtic."

The first tribes of the Celtic group to settle in Europe used the myth, as had the Egyptians and other early peoples, to convey abstract thoughts which could not be presented as clearly and forcefully in words alone. Orpheus, of whose identity we know little, taught the Greeks their mysteries and sacred rites by using myths.

The myth supplied a picture in outward form to suggest and encourage a direct intuitional understanding. The stories, which conveyed cosmic history and charted the whole cycle of the divine unfolding of mankind, were later dramatized annually at the mystery festivals. The usual theme of ancient poets and dramatists dealt with the human soul in its existence on earth, where the hero struggled to conquer animal nature. Variations in events, whether the hero were Ulysses, Orpheus, Hercules, Horus, Buddha, or Jesus, always depicted the pilgrim's progress or the divine Self's journey from earth back to the skies. The myth gave to the unseen abstract truth a physical representation so that the people could understand it.

Modern ignorance of the myth form of literature has led to many misconceptions about ancient beliefs. Primitive man had common sense and did not confuse the myth presentation as literal fact. The Christian, especially, has mistakenly accepted on faith, as historical fact, the allegorical concepts which we know now represent the same great symbolic theme that has been reiterated in many forms.

Myths were produced by the highest types of poetic genius, which traced series of parallels, correspondences, and analogies between the seen and unseen. They skillfully used physical nature to typify spiritual reality. Primitive man was acquainted with the processes of nature from firsthand experience, and the myth form of teaching led him from the known to the unknown. It took great wisdom to show him the corresponding spiritual counterpart within the interior of man himself.

Exalted spiritual and intellectual wisdom fashioned the myths, not a primitive superstitious people. The early people knew only their lower physical world and could not have realized the outer world to be a reflection from the realities of a higher world. Modern educated men have been perplexed for many centuries by these ancient myths. By studying the ancient Egyptian and Greek books they are gaining the keys and learning to comprehend their deep significance and challenge.[30]

During three centuries of the Golden Age, some six hundred Greek philosophers lived who were to change the course of intellectual history. The inquiring mind was challenged to develop abstract thinking by interpreting the divine mystery hidden in the mythical and moral fables. Their "gods" were discovered by experiences in consciousness, not by worship and belief of history as divine. Symbolism challenged the mind to seek an explanation. These great minds sought the spiritual wisdom concealed behind the mysterious veil of their elaborate mythology.

Poets, such as Homer and Hesiod, wrote with imagination and spiritual conviction, but it was the Orphic tradition which broke down the historical materialism of Homer, Hesiod and earlier writings. The Orphic teachings supplied the key to interpret the divine mystery. The result was an expansion in consciousness.

Pythagoras was one of the great leaders in thought. He was born about 590 B.C. in Sidon, Syria not far from Bethlehem. His father was told in a prophecy at Delphi that a son would be born who would greatly benefit mankind. Both Jesus and Pythagoras were said to be "sons of God," not of man. Pythagoras was first influenced by Orphic teachers. When he was grown he traveled extensively. Thales had urged him to go to Egypt, where he remained twenty-five years. It is recorded that he traveled to the farthest parts of the known world—to Babylon, Persia, India; he studied also with Arabs, Chaldeans, and the Druid priests in Gaul. After initiation into some fourteen systems of world religions he recognized that they were all identical in principle, that all acknowledged one God, and that all practiced similar esoteric disciplines. He then established his own school at Crotona, Italy.

Pythagoras emphasized harmony, but it was Heraclitus (540-475) who indicated that harmony is not static but an ever developing relationship between opposites. Change is ordered and universal. A unitary process runs through the variety of nature. This process of continual transformations makes a harmony of opposites.[31]

Pythagoras envisioned moderation in all things: "Nothing in excess." He taught that harmony is a state prerequisite to beauty. He believed there are successive grades of good, ascending from matter to spirit. Life, consciousness, and all things are at different degrees of goodness and harmony. He thought of the universe as a great harmonic ratio between degrees of goodness, the gradations ascending from matter (the least degree) to spirit (the greatest degree) of harmony and beauty. He taught that the Monad, the all inclusive One, is related to each of its manifested parts and that essential growth of each part is toward the Grand Monad, symbolized by the Sun or Central Fire. He considered ten to be the sacred number or the sum of all parts and to represent the completeness of all things.

Pythagoras taught that relationships are essentially mental rather than physical. He stressed the value of friendship as an important ingredient of relationship. He suggested that merging with the spirit of things is more valuable than knowing the forms. The accumulation of knowledge comes in many ways but wisdom consists of understanding the cause or source of things. Wisdom is attained by lifting the intellect to a point of intuitive awareness of the invisible. The ultimate source that man could recognize was the Monad, which has been described as the "mysterious permanent atom of the Pythagorians." Manly Hall has written:

> The God of Pythagoras was the *Monad,* or the One that is Everything. He described God as the Supreme Mind distributed throughout all parts of the universe—the Cause of all things, the Intelligence of all things, and the Power within all things. He further declared the motion of God to be circular, the body of God to be composed of the substance of light, and the nature of God to be composed of the substance of truth.[32]

Plato, born in 427 B.C., about a century after Pythagoras, was said to be the son of Apollo, so great were his talents. He became the disciple of Socrates when he was twenty. Later, with disciples of Pythagoras, he studied the Orphic Mysteries, as did most of the wise thinkers of his time. He visited Egypt and was initiated into some of the mystery schools there. His broad background of inclusive thinking enabled him to express a summary of the noblest and best of Greek philosophy. He was said to be large of heart and body, with capacities for uniting and synthesizing science, religion, arts, and philosophy.

He believed that an all-pervading unity is everywhere present and evident. Unity is reality and truth, and division is an illusion. In his wisdom, he conceived of God, man, and the universe as related fragments in a common unity. Monotheism, or the existence of one Life in which all living things are its segments, made all learning for Plato a study in relationships. Each part is to be examined in its relation to the Whole.

Plato thought of God as Truth and the Reality which sustains the universe. This Truth animates everything. It is the spiritual principle in all of life. Man is the progeny of "the gods," that is, composed inwardly of the spirit of Absolute Truth and composed outwardly of the varying degrees of relative truths which might be called "the gods." He classified men in three divisions:

> The ignorant man is in servitude to his animal nature; the partly informed man is in servitude to his intellectual nature; and the divinely enlightened man is united with his spiritual principle which is the sustaining power in the midst of his being.[33]

Plato was an idealistic philosopher. He reasoned from universals to particulars. He was an abstract thinker, and some records indicate that he had some psychic development. Probably the most important of Plato's writings, yet the least known, are his *Five Books on Theology*. Socrates left no writings, but his convictions are preserved in the Platonic dialogues. Plato viewed reality as seeking freedom in a permanent static harmony. Plato had a mind which synthesized, but his pupil, Aristotle, analyzed and diversified. Aristotle greatly influenced European thought with the idea of a dualism separating the processes of the senses and the permanence of timelessness. This dualism of matter and mind is now being replaced by the unitary process which Heraclitus described as an eternal "Becoming."[34]

A formative process is recognized now in all nature and man is becoming aware of himself in the universal sequence.[35] Focusing on the unity of process places tensions in their right relationship. Tensions and harmony are complementary rhythms in all processes. Man is learning to be receptive of the moment-to-moment transformations without preconceived static security or harmony. He moves with the processes of nature, not struggling against them.

Some Orphic and Platonic expressions of unity are:

> God is Truth, and the light his shadow.[36]

> Love is the eldest and noblest and mightiest of the gods and the chiefest author and giver of virtue in life and of happiness after death.[37]

> God being a luminous principle, residing in the midst of the most subtle fire, he remains forever invisible to the eyes of those who do not elevate themselves above material life. . . .[38]

> God geometrizes, and His government of the world is no less mathematically exact than His creation of it.[39]

> What God is, I know not: What He is not, I know.[40]

Hebraic and Christian Concepts of Unity

The best known of the Christian literature is the Bible, made up of the Old and New Testaments. This "canonized" collection of writings is accepted by each division of Christendom, by Roman Catholic, Greek Orthodox and Protestant groups. The Old Testament is also used as scriptures for Judaism and for the Islamic religion.

The Jewish Old Testament, written in ancient Hebrew or related Chaldean and Aramaic languages, consists of a large number of books. The earliest complete manuscripts of the Old Testament which have been found date from the ninth or tenth century A.D. The Dead Sea Scrolls included a complete manuscript of Isaiah believed to have been written in the first or second century B.C. The Old Testament was written over a period of time which extended from early barbarous days characterized by bloody sacrifices to much later periods notable for higher nobler concepts and grander understanding of a Divine Being. Some of the books contain most exalted passages concerning the nature of God and ideals of righteousness. The Psalms, like the *Vedas* of the Indians and the *Gathas* of the Zoroastrians, are song-poems marked by most elevated and noble spirit, but some writings from earlier periods are exceedingly militant and not elevated. A large part of the Old Testament was written in historical form, and unfortunately it has been accepted by orthodox Christianity as literal history instead of as a great allegory written in historical form. It repeats in many ways the plan for man's evolution.

Some of the early Old Testament writings described the Supreme Deity as a cruel despot, both ruthless and arrogant. There are many passages that are incredible, quite impossible, and immoral. Early scholars confused the allegorical style of the ancient writings, interpreting it as literal fact, because they did not yet have the keys to its symbolic interpretation. As a result, institutions grew that fostered narrowness, declared the impossible to be true fact, and maintained that the entire writing was a divinely inspired record of literal truth.

The New Testament consists of four Gospels that give the life of the founder of the religion; some epistles, written by his followers, that give an account of the early church; and a book of prophecy. It is a collection of oral traditions selected late in the second century. It contains a large number of the teachings of the Christ which are more ethical than philosophical. There is little of doctrine in the gospels; instructions addressed to advanced disciples were suppressed by the Church Fathers. Most of the dogmatic statements are contained in the epistles, which give an outline of the faith.

The Book of Wisdom and other apocryphal scriptures of the Jews show great spiritual wisdom. Some of these are placed between the Old and New Testaments in the Roman Catholic Bibles but usually are omitted in the Protestant Bibles.

The Bible is a valid part of the ancient wisdom and is not to be shielded as a distinct authority but is to be studied with keen insight and criticism as is any other contribution to understanding. Jesus, a superlative character, influences our lives as the divinity within. It is the "fullness of Christ" that "lighteth every man that cometh into the world." It is the search for the Higher Self which challenges modern man, who does not rely on historical events of one period but who seeks universal truths.

In order to understand the growth of Christianity, one should study the large mass of apocryphal writings which are never bound with the Bible. They are most interesting stories of primitive Christianity, of the early church, of the infancy of Jesus, of his later life, of his work in invisible worlds, and of his followers. There is also a large mass of literature written by learned teachers, bishops, and Fathers of the Church during the second, third, fourth, and fifth centuries, showing growth in metaphysical and philosophical understanding.

The history as given in the scriptures appealed to the simple-minded, but such people often overlooked the absurdities that had been introduced to indicate hidden symbolic significances. The more educated interpreted the symbolic meaning. The Christian wisdom was not secret, but only those who were prepared to understand could comprehend the higher challenges.

As the Roman Empire spread, the ignorant masses in Europe dominated the religion. For their benefit the Church emphasized faith rather than knowledge. Gradually the spiritual truths understood by the few enlightened were submerged. Later in the Protestant countries the policy of teaching the ignorant and immature drove out those with capacities for wider, deeper insights. The Christian Church was thus weakened. Skepticism developed and those capable of intellectual insight abandoned a teaching which contradicted simple scientific facts.

Early Christianity in the West was focused upon development of vigorous, young nations. The people, full of energy and strength, needed an appropriate training. Jesus gave few subtle metaphysical teachings but much about ethics, morality, and practical spiritual living. Perhaps the reason for this was that the people to whom he brought the message of brotherhood were fierce, cruel, and jealously resentful of his purity and compassion.

The gospel of love and compassion spread among the poor as the early Church developed, but at the same time the struggle between knowledge and ignorant superstition increased. The Gnostic scholars tried to teach the masses the wisdom of the East under new names. One of the greatest treasures of ancient Christian occultism, the *Pistis Sophia,* was written at this time, and also the *Divine Pymander* (described earlier). But the narrow, ignorant ones who were in control considered as heretics those with the wisdom of the ages and persecuted them. The Dark Ages followed and the doctrines were twisted and distorted. Wisdom, however, was preserved under the guise of alchemy and astrology and by various secret societies.

The early Church retained enough true religion to elevate the heart. Many people learned of love and sacrifice by devotion to a personal Christ. However, their intellects were not trained by philosophy and metaphysics to understand the larger, more universal concepts which had characterized the ancient religions.

Early twentieth century Christianity failed to develop people whose ideals of right human conduct could cope with international problems. There have been international attempts to better human conditions and attempts to solve problems without wars. Communication and transportation technologies have increased universal understanding. The far reaching findings in the various fields of science indicate progress and an unfolding plan.

A new direction of development is becoming evident in the latter part of the twentieth century. Along with the lawlessness, sensuality, and artificial standards of living there are also unparalleled charities and sacrificial efforts in numerous occupational fields. The youth trained in scientific analysis and understanding reject illogical, glamorous, artificial ceremonies. They search for direct methods for the betterment of mankind and of their own lives. Many youths are interested in man's latent potentials and are willing to strive to develop these capacities in themselves in order to better mankind.

Everything in life is related, if the mind is clear to see it, for life is the impersonal, primary relationship between the two poles of attraction and repulsion. The heart relationship of compassion and brotherhood is an expression of this attraction principle and is basic to our existence. Man, at this time, has not learned to use wisely the ever shifting equilibrium in this relationship.

Our universe is indicated by the ancient students as a totality, the Heavenly Man, extending through and reflected in the little man, the microcosm. Man has been described as the "growing point" of all the lower forms of evolutionary development, as all forms progress through various stages toward his capacities. Man has passed through each stage and has acquired individuality by natural impulse or self-directed effort to ascending degrees of intelligence. Man is given no privileges and no gifts except those he earns, since he must pass through each stage. He reaches the stage of self-determination or the man-stage as a summary of earlier experience in the lower stages. He reaches the divine through individual achievement in this man-pattern.

Christianity is entering a new phase of development, world-wide in scope, accepting the good contributions from each nation and each modern or ancient religion. We are outgrowing many of the characteristics common to nineteenth century Christianity such as dogmatic sectarianism, proselytizing, ignorance of the grandeur in ancient scriptures, and intolerant persecutions of those whose form of worship differs from our own.

Religious and scientific concepts are uniting again as it is recognized that the world is not made by random energies but by the power within the totality of being. Physicists found as they broke the atom into smaller and smaller particles that within each minute fragment is similar capacity. Each particle, no matter how small, can with proper combination be formed into any other product. This oneness inherent in every fragment proves, by modern technology, the teachings that the ancient wise men gave earlier peoples in myths and symbols.

The way we describe these concepts—the semantics, terminology, and the descriptive forms used—still confuse and separate people. But since belief in the inherent oneness has now been replaced by technological proof, science and religion merge again to help people understand the basic unity, the immutable oneness expressed in a changing world.

A Christianity is emerging with a trans-sectarian attitude. It is based upon the contributions of the past but adds a unique universal concept. The recognition that all people and all religions come from the same Source is more universally accepted than at any previous time. The concept of One God, unmanifested yet out of whom all forms of manifestation evolve, is one way of expressing a unitive formation. Those of a scientific mind find this same understanding by the proven similarity within each atomic particle. Gradually this wisdom is uniting the consciousness of mankind. International religious groups, both traditional and occult, are organizing to unite peoples' efforts and understandings. Christianity is yet in its infancy. The great ancient plan for the development of all life is still unfolding.

Hebrew Expressions of Unity

> God the Lord, he that created the heavens and stretched them out, he that spread forth the earth, and that which cometh out of it; he that giveth breath unto the people upon it, and spirit to them that walk therein.[41]

> The Lord God is a sun and shield: the Lord will give grace and glory:[42]

> Sun of righteousness, risen, with healing in his wings.[43]

Christian Expressions of Unity

In the beginning was the Word, and the Word was with God, and the Word was God. The same was in the beginning with God. All things were made by him; and without him was not anything made that was made. In him was life; and the life was the light of men. And the light shineth in darkness; and the darkness comprehendeth it not.[44]

God is light, and in him is no darkness at all.[45]

I am the light of the world; he that followeth me shall not walk in darkness, but shall have the light of life.[46]

I am come a light into the world, that whosoever believeth on me should not abide in darkness.[47]

While ye have the light, believe in the light, that ye may be the children of light.[48]

Then shall the righteous shine forth as the sun in the kingdom of their Father.[49]

There is one body, and one Spirit, even as also ye were called in one hope of your calling; one Lord, one faith, one baptism, one God and Father of all, who is over all, and through all, and in all.[50]

REFERENCES

[1] J. Krishnamurti, *Talks in Europe 1965* (Ojai, California: Krishnamurti Writings Inc., 1965), p. 94.

[2] Annie Besant, *Translation of the Bhagavad Gita* (London: Theosophical Publishing Society, 1904) p. 7.

[3] Annie Besant, *Four Great Religions* (Chicago: The Theosophical Press, 1897) p. 25. Mundakopanishad, II., ii., 9.

[4] *Ibid.*, p. 16. Mundakopanishad, II., ii., 10.

[5] *Ibid.*, p. 17. Shvetashvataropanishad, IV., 18, 19, 20.

[6] Swami Paramananda, *The Upanishad* Vol. I (Boston, Mass.: The Vendanta Center, 1919) pp. 28-29. Ish Upanishad IV, V, VI.

[7] Manly P. Hall, *The Noble Eightfold Path* (Los Angeles, California: Philosophical Research Society, 1937) p. 33.

[8] Manly P. Hall, *The Arhats of Buddhism* Part II (Los Angeles, California: Philosophical Research Society, 1953) p. 22.

[9] Houston Smith, *The Religions of Man* (New York, N.Y.: Harper and Row, 1964) p. 158.

[10] *Ibid.*, p. 182.

[11] *Ibid.*, p. 183.

[12] Manly P. Hall, *Twelve World Teachers* (Los Angeles, California: The Philosophers Press, 1937) p. 142.

[13] *Ibid.*, p. 143.

[14] Howard Murphet, "What God Died?," *The American Theosophist,* Spring 1967, p. 126.

[15] *Ibid.*, p. 126.

[16] Annie Besant, *Seven Great Religions* (Adyar, Madras, India: The Theosophical Publishing House, 1966) p. 249.

[17] Hall, *op. cit.*, p. 32.

[18] *Ibid.*, p. 34.

[19] Manly P. Hall, *The Secret Teachings of All Ages* (Los Angeles, California: The Philosophical Research Society Press, 1945) p. XL. (Citing "The Vision of Poimandres of the Divine Pymander.")

[20] Hall, *op. cit., Twelve World Teachers*, p. 42.

[21] Walter, W. G., *The Living Brain* (W. W. Norton & Co., New York, N.Y., 1953) p. 61.

[22] Besant, *op. cit., Four Great Religions,* pp. 58-59 (citing H. P. Blavatsky "Article on Zoroastrianism," *The Theosophist,* IV, p. 224).

[23] *Ibid.*, p. 56, citing Ormazd Yasht, trans. from A. H. Bleek.

[24] *Ibid.*, pp. 56-57, citing Gatha Ahunavaiti.

[25] Hall, *op. cit., Secret Teachings of All Ages,* p. CLXXXIX.

[26] Besant, *op. cit., Seven Great Religions,* p. 214.

[27] Manly P. Hall, *Horizon Magazine,* Spring 1951, p. 37.

[28] Besant, *op. cit., Seven Great Religions,* p. 228.

[29] Howard Murphet, "What God Died?," *The American Theosophist,* Spring 1967, p. 126.

[30] Alvin Boyd Kuhn, *The Lost Light* (New York, N.Y.: Columbia University, 1940) pp. 67-72.

[31] Lancelot Whyte, *The Next Development in Man* (New York, N.Y.: The New American Library, 1962), p. 154.

[32] Hall, *op. cit., Secret Teachings of All Ages,* p. LXVI.

[33] Hall, *op. cit., Twelve World Teachers,* p. 153.

[34] Whyte, *op. cit.*, p. 154.

[35] *Ibid.*, p. 199.

[36] Hall, *op. cit.*, p. 160.

[37] *Ibid.*, p. 161.

[38] Hall, *op. cit., Secret Teachings of All Ages,* p. XXXI citing Porphyry.

[39] Hall, *op. cit., Twelve World Teachers,* p. 161.

[40] Manly P. Hall, *Journey in Truth* (Los Angeles, California: Philosophical Research Society, 1945), p. 105.

[41] Isa. 42:5.

[42] Ps. 84:11.

[43] Mal. 4:2.

[44] John 1:1-6.
[45] I John 1:7.
[46] John 8:12.
[47] John 12:46.
[48] John 12:36.
[49] Matt. 13:43.
[50] Eph. 4:5-6.

Chapter 2

THE TRINITY

Most religions reiterate that the one unmanifested Source expresses or manifests itself in many ways. Three general characteristics or aspects of this One are variously named by different cultures, but although the names differ the triune classifications seem similar.

If life is to progress from the primary unity and to multiply itself, the initial division must be of itself. The One gave Itself to division and limitation, yet each part remained an integral unit of the total. And so it was said that God, the One, lived in the parts and the parts lived in Him. In the heart of each fragment was hidden the Lord of Divine Life, and life became ever more Self-conscious inasmuch as there was nothing of which to be conscious but Itself.

Intuitional understandings of the ancient seers anticipated the scientific objective knowledge of relationships between life and the universe.[1] The Godhead was early associated as a Spirit within the sun, known as the "Spiritual Sun." The sun made a good nature-symbol for all the people. First, it remained one intact ball of fire as it traveled through space. Second, it generated light which is like the fire of the sun yet not the fire. And third, it radiated active energy to all living things. The Spiritual Sun manifested as the sun, as light, and as creative energy. This trinity became closely associated in the people's everyday activities, although many ways or attributes were used in describing them.

Someone has set forth "be-ness, becoming, and being" as the source, method, and goal in a trinity that describes everyday functioning. Be-ness, the absolute boundless Principle; becoming, the harmony of nature or interrelationship of life and form or brotherhood; and being, the goal of all manifested life.

The Hindu Trinity

A Hindu may think of philosophy or religion as he pleases. His training encourages freedom of opinion. This freedom gradually produced a vast number of sects and beliefs in India, yet the early teachers had basic knowledge of the invisible worlds. Their purpose in religious training was to bring the masses to an understanding of these invisible values and of the individual's duty toward them.

The training also most carefully detailed social life and family life with set orthodox rules and customs. The conduct thus imposed in daily affairs helped each person learn to live harmoniously with other men and with his environment. Such a regulated way of life stabilized evolution in its early stages. Duty to God and duty to one's fellow men were emphasized. Man and wife were drawn together by spiritual affinity rather than by desires of the flesh. They were joined for spiritual development and were required to participate in social rituals together.

The ancient *Vedas,* with their profound wisdom and varied concepts, stimulated intellectual development. They taught that Brahman is the impersonal creative principle in the universe. The Supreme Brahman, the unmanifested God, is concealed as the inmost Self in every being. Brahman, by self-limitation, gradually causes the visible universe to come into being. Then eventually all existence will be reabsorbed into Brahman. Without Brahman there is no life, no thought, no mind.

For purposes of worship the one Brahman is expressed in threefold personified form as Brahma, Vishnu, and

Shiva. Brahma, the creative aspect through whose meditation all things are produced, is universal mind, the divine Chit. Vishnu, the All-Pervader, the sustaining life of God present in every atom of the universe, is the dual aspect of Ananda. Shiva, the Regenerator and the Destroyer, liberating the life within the form in order that it might take higher expression, is Sat.

Brahman is hidden within these names and classifications, ever uniting them. The quality of Sat started as pure existence in the unmoving mineral kingdom, but Chit and Ananda qualities were concealed in this kingdom also. In the vegetable kingdom the dual principle (initial phases of pleasure and pain) unfolded; this, in later evolution, would develop into Ananda qualities. In the animal kingdom is found the beginning of the qualities of Chit, but with the other two qualities concealed.

As animal and man evolve all three qualities develop, and at the end of man's evolution Sat, Chit, and Ananda characteristics will be fully developed and man will become Brahman.[2] Man will know that the Self of the Universe and his own Self are One. The elaborate Hindu rites and ceremonies were at first formulated to help ignorant man realize his visible and invisible environments and how they were related. All forms are to be understood as outward expressions of the thoughts of living intelligences, whether they are in dense or more subtle matter. Each individual is part of the Eternal One.

As men reached more advanced understandings, six religious schools developed. By various methods each school taught its aspirants how to attain union (yoga) with God. Each taught that only the One is eternal; that all but Brahman is illusion, inasmuch as every limited form of expression is changing; that the universe is but God's thoughts expressed in forms, so that all forms are one and not separate. It is the Self within the form that is important, the living, evolving consciousness.

Each worshiper understands the one God in proportion to his own degree of development. The varied approaches and the many types of worship gradually prepare the people to seek the one Supreme Lord of the universe. The worshipers are taught to recognize every action as a sacrifice to the Supreme God, although it might be dedicated to one of the Trinity or to lesser gods.

The Buddhist Trinity

The human race was greatly blessed by the birth of Gautama Buddha for, though he was born in India, his influence transcends all racial and national limitations. His reasonable and logical viewpoints about daily living and his keen evaluation of the purposes and responsibilities of life even now, in the twentieth century, challenge Christians and Buddhists alike.

His life can be studied historically as that of Prince Siddartha, born about 623 B.C., who struggled with the religious intolerances and social conditions of his times and who tried to reform the corrupt practices which had crept into Hinduism. He brought much hope to the ignorant and the poor by teaching them of immortality and by giving them a goal in life.

Even more challenging is a study of his life as part of the great cosmic myth pattern which is repeated so frequently in the world religions. We are told of his preparation through hundreds of rebirths into lives of sacrifice and devotion, before his last life on earth. The Prince was led from earthly manhood to the exalted position of a Bodhisattva (one who serves humanity) and eventually to that of Buddhahood and perfect illumination.

The Lord Gautama's pilgrimage in search for wisdom shows the possibilities in the life of every individual to find the "golden robe" or the radiant consciousness of great beauty. The Prince was surrounded by every luxury, but he renounced a kingdom and all personal desires in order to serve humanity. In a vision or experience his attention was focused upon problems of age, sickness, and death but also upon a vision of an ascetic, one serene, calm, and full of peace and happiness. These contrasts haunted him, so he set out alone and penniless, leaving his kingdom, a beautiful wife, and a son.

Wherever he journeyed he asked why people grew old, what caused illness, and what death was. No one could give him satisfactory answers, but the great need of the people kept him searching. The holy men argued and philosophized, but he decided that mere intellectual knowing could not cure the sorrows of men. For six years he tried their methods of penances, reducing his food intake until he fell emaciated. Then he went on his way alone, still meditating. At Gaya, while meditating under the sacred Asvattha (Bodhi) tree, temptations of pain and pleasure constantly tested his resolution.

Finally the light came to him. His mind approached the Eternal, and he lost all desire. He knew then the cause of sorrow, and that its cure was to rise above all desire only thus to find peace. He understood that for himself and for mankind this was the way to the all-inclusive peace called "Nirvana." While in this state he learned of the "chain of causation" and traced the evolution of the universe, expressing it in the twelve *Nidanas*. Between the extremes of self-mortification and self-indulgence he saw the middle path which leads to peace, knowledge, and Nirvana. (This is called the "Noble Eightfold Path." It will be detailed later.) Freed from all illusion and perfect in understanding and wisdom, he taught his moral philosophy for more than forty-five years. He believed the mystery of being could be understood by recognizing the two laws of karma and rebirth. He became known as the "Blessed One" and has been acclaimed one of the greatest of the humanitarians, religious reformers, and servants to humanity.

Buddhism teaches its followers to regard the life of Buddha as an illustration that the evolution of consciousness changes the human body by spiritual processes. Buddha wandered, ever seeking truth, always striving to master the powers of nature, searching in the lower worlds for the wisdom to climb upward to spiritual mountains. Changes in the body, mind, and spirit, a three-stranded cord, gave outward expression to a consciousness glowing with the radiance of ever-increasing development until even the atmosphere around him came to be like a halo or golden garment.

Gautama's disciples were Hindu people who accepted the ancient trinity in which Brahman, the one invisible Source, manifested as Brahma in the First Aspect, as Vishnu in the Second Aspect, and as Shiva in the Third Aspect. Gautama did not emphasize these accepted metaphysical concepts nor the changelessness of Reality, but he did emphasize the need for changes in individual consciousness, changes in body and mind, and he taught his pupils how to achieve such changes—through meditation and service to others.

The three jewels or trinity of Buddhism are: the Buddha, the Dhamma, and the Sangha. The Buddha is the Enlightened One, the great teacher of compassion. The Dhamma is the teaching of the Buddha, or the Law. The Sangha is the collective name for followers of the Buddha (Bhikkus) who renounce worldly pursuits and spend their lives in study, practice and dissemination of the Dhamma. Esoterically the term Sangha is also used in relation to those who have reached the Arhat level, or liberation.

The Egyptian Hermetic Trinity

The Egyptian astronomers considered the sun the most important celestial body in the heavens. It became for them the symbol of the Supreme Creative Authority, the One Light. The concept of the Trinity, the Eternal One seen as three, corresponded to the powers and principles of the sun. First, they noted that the sun set or "died" each night but rose again the next morning; this made it a fitting symbol of immortality for them. Second, the astronomers noted the sun's annual passage through the twelve celestial houses of the heavens, staying in each thirty days. Third, they noted the path of the sun called the "precession of the equinoxes." It retrogrades around the zodiac through the twelve signs at the rate of one degree every seventy-two years. In their allegorical language, the sun was said to assume the nature of the living creature in each zodiacal sign while passing through the sign. The Solar Fire, traveling through the twelve houses of the zodiac, was also thought to perform twelve essential benevolent labors for the human race.

The philosophers noted also three distinct daily phases of the sun: rising, midday, and setting. The symbol of light, God, Creator of the world, was represented by the sunrise phase; God, the one sent out across the world, was the Son, shown by the midday phase; and corresponding to the Holy Spirit was the sunset phase, after which the sun wandered in the lower worlds of activity. The visible sun personified the Spiritual Sun in three classifications of its functioning.

The Egyptian God Osiris has been considered by some as the positive universal life agent, and Isis, the great Mother Goddess, as representing the active temporal institutions of the mysteries and priesthood, or the Third Aspect of the Trinity. Horus, their son, manifested the dual characteristics of the Second Aspect of the Trinity. Typhon was the power in the physical universe constantly seeking to destroy spiritual values.

The ancient Egyptians were a highly civilized and gifted people. They were well informed and had long been trained in the mysteries of subjective thought. Their priests knew the seven liberal sciences. They experimented with animal and mineral magnetism, the lodestone, forces of psychological impressions, reading the inmost secrets of the soul, and sending their own spiritual force out from the body. They were masters of mesmerism, clairvoyance, and electro-biology. They used herbs and drugs and employed music and resonance. They could imitate precious stones by chemical processes. They employed engineering skills to change the course of the Nile and to quarry, shape, and place huge building stones with mathematical precision. They established ethical codes which other nations adopted. Their metaphysics perceived the relation of causes and effects. Their philosophy abolished the terrifying power of death. They realized that life depended upon an invisible energy, both in man and in the universe, and that the unmanifested power produced the objective universe.

Although the Egyptians have been accused of superstition, their beliefs were not contrary to Nature. Instead the Egyptians had great knowledge of natural laws, and their "magic" was knowledge of superphysical laws. They believed in both visible and invisible powers at work in Nature. Many natural truths are beyond sense perception and elude us, but the Egyptians believed that every phenomenon, physical or superphysical, was related to laws of cause and effect that could be examined and classified.[3]

Aknaton, known in history as Amen-Hotep IV, King of Upper and Lower Egypt, was born in 1388 B.C. The young pharaoh learned to honor within himself an ever-present Spirit, the "Sun behind the sun." His sense of Spiritual Light, ever flowing to the birds and insects, to the poor and the rich, to enemies as well as to his countrymen, enabled him to establish a new social order in an effort to re-establish the ancient teachings and to overcome a corrupt priesthood.

Meditating upon the cosmic significance of the Sun as the Universal Father, he envisioned and then established, for a brief period in history, a true brotherhood. His convictions were overpowered after a reign of sixteen years. Yet at this early date in history, thirteen hundred years before the birth of Christ, he applied the principle of political democracy and women's suffrage, settled internal disputes by arbitration, and refused to go to war against invaders of his kingdom because he regarded all as the children of the Sun and therefore his brothers. He replaced the local deities with a universal concept. He believed the Spiritual Sun to be everywhere, so even those who died remained ever in the Light.[4]

In his new capital city, Aknaton erected a temple to the Formless One. He realized, while meditating, that the one God was no tribal deity but a Universal Essence. The solar disc was chosen as the visible symbol of this universal Force. Carvings in stone of the rays of the sun ending with human hands indicated to his people the Active Aspect of God, the hand of God in all things. The light of the sun was the "Giver of Life" to the people. The ever-present Spirit was in all things. Aknaton recognized the triple aspects of deity. He had the moral strength to sacrifice wealth, honor, position, and life itself rather than compromise ethical principles. His dream of a government that is based upon the ideal of love yet challenges mankind.

The Zoroastrian Trinity

Zoroastrianism and Hinduism both stretch back into the night of time. Students find evidence that the Persian prophets derived their teachings from the same line as the Hindu teachings. There may have been a number of prophets called Zoroaster or Zarathushtra. The scanty records now available confuse and merge the characteristics of these teachers. The teachings continually stressed purity in every relation and in every action. Modern archeological excavations and newly found cuneiform writings continue to yield data about these teachings.

The ancient Persians were an agricultural people, and

much of their religion centered around astronomy and sciences related to their work. They considered the planets moving about the sun and the stars lighting the night sky to be spiritual intelligences influencing all life. Each living intelligence moved in changeless order, guided by unswerving will and perfect wisdom. Their sacred literature established "Zeroana Akerna," the One Existence, unmanifested in "Boundless Time." The sacrifice and limitation of this One caused the manifestation of Ahura Mazda or Ormazd, the "King of Life."

Ahura Mazda, the "first-born," from whom all proceed, was the first Person of their Trinity. Two principles had their root in Him, and between these two poles the universe was formed. From reality and nonreality, or from light and darkness, came the many. "The Increaser" was ever giving life; "The Destroyer" was the material side which broke up in order that life might express in higher forms. These twin forces (Spenta Mainyush and Angio Mainyush) are everywhere present in the Divine Being, forming the second Person in the manifested Trinity; Armaiti, Intelligence and Mind, is the third Person.

Dastur F. A. Bode speaks of a trinity formed of Ahura Mazda, Spenta Mainyu, and Fravashi. The whole universe came from Ahura Mazda, the loving Father, or the Source. In the process of cosmic evolution all will eventually become like Him and return to Him.[5] The teachings stress Self-unfolding or perpetual regeneration of the spirit of man. This is a continual resurrection taking place all the time. By intuitive, unitive knowledge Spenta Mainya—the Holy transcendent Spirit, the Christ within—draws the soul of man toward conscious Reality or Ahura Mazda. Fravashi—the pure total Self in man—guides and inspires him to perceptive, intuitive wisdom and illumination.

Fire, the symbol of Divine Life, was sometimes called the "Son of Ahura Mazda." Fire, the supreme emblem for glory, the living flame, gave the universe. Fire and the varying rhythms are also thought to symbolize the subtle differences and interrelationships between the many planes of manifestation. In one of the early traditional oracles Zarathushtra spoke:

> When thou beholdest a sacred Fire, formless, flashing dazzlingly throughout the world, Hear thou the voice of the Fire.[6]

Zarathushtra was described as standing near an altar raising his rod, which was used in the mysteries, and living fire was said to descend to the altar and round about him. The ancient teaching was that in early times the sacred fire was called down from the "Akasha" at the words of the priest as a living symbol of God.

The modern religion of the Parsi carries on many traditions which were taught by Zarathushtra. Although this group is small in number their emphasis on purity, with fire as its symbol, has influenced many of the people in west-central Asia and elsewhere.

The Orphic Greek Trinity

Orpheus was usually described as the son of the god Apollo. Allegorically this meant that Apollo, as Light, spread beauty and truth and wisdom. Calliope, the mother of Orpheus, supplied the vehicle for his incarnation and prepared him for earth life by teaching him of harmony and beauty. Orpheus brought music and perfection of form wherever he traveled. This description signified that Orpheus was an initiate, one of the seers who had knowledge of the heavenly worlds but whose home, for a brief time, would be wandering on the earth.

Orpheus taught that all existence came from one immeasurable Good Principle, the one Cause.

> God is revealed as an Eternally Abiding Good, an Ever Flowing Fountain of Truth and Law, an Omnipotent Unity, an Omniscient Realty. In this inter-

> pretation, Deity is not a being, but a source of beings; not light but the source of light; not mind, but the source of mind; the hidden origin of all revealed things.[7]

From this immeasurable Source emerged a triad of qualities: Being, Life, and Intellect. "That which subsists upon itself" manifested in the First Aspect as Eternal Being. Life was the Second Aspect, and Intellect was the Third Aspect. Each of these was further divided into a trinity, each of which was imbued with the similar qualities of Being, Life, and Intellect.

The Supreme Demiurgos and His progeny, the original Titans, fashioned the supermundane, the liberated, and the mundane spheres. The Second Aspect of the Creative Triad was worshiped by the people and called the Demiurgos. The Third Aspect of the Creative Triad was personified as Zeus, Poseidon, and Hades; these established spirit, soul, and form in the material universe. Zeus, as the father, ruled over air, water, and earth; he was lord of the atmosphere, winds, sky, and breath. Poseidon ruled the streams, the oceans, and the creatures that lived in them. Hades ruled the earth, the subterranean deep caverns, and mountains; he represented the creative power in all physical elements of nature. All physical creations, seers taught, were imprisoned in a body-form. The story of Orpheus journeying in the underworld to find the imprisoned form of Eurydice, symbolized man's search for experience, soul power, and understanding.

Pythagoras taught, "All things consist of three." Everything in nature was divisible into three parts. Every problem could be diagrammed as a triangle. The universe was divided into the Supreme World, the Superior World, and the Inferior World.

The Supreme World which interpenetrated all was the home of deity. This deity, considered omnipresent, omnipotent, and omniscient, pervaded the two lower worlds. The Superior world was the home of superhuman men, the immortals. Also, the archetypes, or the nature and plan of all beings and things, dwelt in this Superior World. Pythagoras indicated that each form was an imprint in physical substance of its archetype. The Greeks called these archetypes the "shadows" which were cast into the lower material world of form. The third or Inferior World was the home of all material entities, of the mortal gods, the demiurgos, the angels, daemons, mankind, and the lower kingdoms.

The Greeks considered the triangle a sacred sign. It symbolized the One, the Monad, "Sire of God and man," or the Divine Father. It was the whole or sum of the parts in a unit. The duad was a symbol of polarity or the Great Mother. The triad made of these two symbolized that God gave birth to his worlds. The One was an androgynous symbol and became the creative aspect when it divided into the duad which was capable of becoming parent of progeny. The circle was the greatest of all polygons consisting of an infinitude of sides. A trinity in the circle was complete with the center, radius, and circumference. The threefold symbol of the triangle indicated the spiritual body, whereas the fourfold symbols were used for material forms. Socrates also taught that nature was threefold: the One, the Beautiful, and the Good. Plato spoke of a threefold nature with Unity as the Source of all.

The Christian Trinity

Christianity, or "The Way," as taught by the first Apostles, quickly absorbed most of the mystery schools of that day because the "Christian mysteries" were essentially the same teachings. The Supreme Deity is available in the pure, quiet depths of each form of life. Man's mental interests and his material, fleshly desires incessantly drown out his divinity. Yet the seed, the infant deity, slumbers within his heart. "The kingdom of heaven" and "hope of glory" are within his consciousness.

The wholeness of God is not present in man; only a potential ray is projected into every man's nature. Each creature is apportioned the measure he is capable of receiving. The nucleus of divinity is implanted as a seed of Divine Being. This divine seed implanted in man is the Christos. Paul saw clearly that a portion of God was in each. He tried to clarify the confusion by crying, "Know ye not your own selves, how that Jesus Christ is within you?"

Deity is not at some far off distance as many have believed. We are born with that potential and it is present at all times within us. We may be ignorant, if that is sin, but we are a portion of God. No religious organization bestows this potential. It is innate in all forms of consciousness. We are already "Sons of God."

Alvin B. Kuhn has pointed out[8] the grave materialistic confusion brought about by mistranslating the Greek "monogenes" as "only begotten" instead of the translation meaning "born of one parent only." The ancient teaching emphasized that human beings develop spiritually from the potential of deity within themselves. For Christendom, the unfortunate mistranslation has emphasized the power of Spirit as if it is something given from an outside Source. This confusion also led to the misconception of another Being paying our debts, as if someone else could sacrifice to cancel our mistakes. Shifting responsibility is always easy, but it has pauperized religion as it does society.

The ancient seers called the One Essence "God" and to make it clearer for the masses the portions of deity which functioned as powers were recognized by many names as "the Gods" or "the gods." This distinction has been lost in the translation of the Bible, using only the term "God" for both concepts.

The ancient myths and folklore presented spiritual realities under the guise of picturesque nature stories. Primitive man was taught subjective truths by parable that suggested correspondences and analogies between things seen and unseen. Their deities were personifications of principles, not persons. The practice of belittling myths and folklore, believing them to represent ignorant superstition, has robbed Christian society of hidden depths of much spiritual wisdom.

We still understand but little of the symbolic theology hidden in alchemy, astrology, and ancient philosophy. For instance, the religious myths repeatedly state that the Sun Gods, Messiahs, all had two mothers. A key in the Egyptian *Book of the Dead* states, "Isis conceived him, Nephthys gave him birth." The mysteries taught that life was spiritually conceived but materially born.

It may be remembered how Nicodemus asked about the statement "Ye must be born again," and Jesus replied that a man "must be born of water and the Spirit." The ancients used the symbols of water and earth for the physical ideas, and the symbols of air and fire for spiritual concepts. Heraclitus stated: "Man is a portion of cosmic fire, imprisoned in a body of earth and water." Plato said of man: ". . . through body it is an animal; through intellect it is a god." Man could comprehend the spiritual within only when his evolution had advanced enough for his higher spiritual part to control his lower nature.

The old parables and myths expressed the concept that life, the essence of deity, was multiplied, that is, broken into an infinite number of fragments and distributed to a multitude of creatures. This is exemplified in the miracle of the loaves and fishes in the Christian Gospels, the people having fasted for three days (meaning they had evolved through three kingdoms). The "three days" symbolize a period of time, in this case the period required for development of mineral, vegetable, and animal kingdoms. These people had been deprived of spiritual food because they were not ready until they were given the many fragments of bread (the symbol of material development) and the fishes (the symbol of spiritual development). It was only after these three periods of development that man became ready for the evolution in which the spiritual or Christos could be born in man.

The ignorant masses, yearning for social betterment, flocked into the Christian churches. Many hoped quickly to escape their low economic state but were not interested in slow spiritual evolution. The unrest of the masses fomented a widespread rebellion against aristocracy, culture, and wisdom. Early in church history the Church Fathers recast the Gospels making them a human, historical biography of one person, instead of the symbolic, mythical portrayal of man's total experience in evolution. The Roman revolt against the spiritual mystery teachings also suppressed universal wisdom and supplanted it with a materialistic idea of a personal Messiah.

As Christianity spread to the uneducated and downtrodden, it lost much of its former wisdom. The suppression of knowledge and wisdom hastened the "Dark Ages." The Church Fathers emphasized the ancient concept of the germinal deity in man, but they limited it to the historical Jesus rather than applying it to all men. They were competing with so-called "pagan" religions and were proselytizing. They did not yet realize that all religions evolve from the same Source, and that each of the great religions contributes its unique additions to the evolving world understandings.

Christians describe the Universal Deity by a triple classification which is personified and called "The Father," "The Son," and the "Holy Spirit." Power or Will is unlimited in the Father but in man is only gradually developed as he desires and as he is impelled to action. Wisdom or self-consciousness is limited in man as self-realization. When man realizes his own divinity, only then is the "Christ Aspect" born in the human Spirit, only then is he "One with the Son." Man expresses this Second Aspect of "The Son" as love, the cohesive element which tries to unite and bring together separating forces. The Third Aspect of the Trinity, called the "Holy Spirit," is Creative Intelligence. Man expresses it in the world with his intellect by creating form. His mental faculties such as imagination, memory, anticipation, and inductive and deductive reasoning bring him gradually to more direct intuition and truth through action.

Each person shows the Spirit in three aspects: by will power, wisdom, and the creative activity of intellect. In man the aspect of will functions as self-determination, the aspect of wisdom functions as intuition, and the aspect of intellect functions as mind and intelligence. Each of these spiritual forces is expressed in a variety of ways in the physical world. The Self, as a spiritual intelligence, uses or works in many kinds of "matter." Every emotional mood, every change in consciousness, sets up different frequencies in the materials in which the Self functions.[9] The Self is not these changing functions, moods, or insights. The Self is a spiritual intelligence, the reality, which uses the subtle functions, moods, and insights.

Gradually, during a long period of evolution, man is unfolding his capacities. The three aspects of divinity in man are as yet in embryonic form, but each life experience in the world should help man grow toward the characteristics of the Divine Trinity.

REFERENCES

[1] Michel Gauquelin, *The Cosmic Clocks* (Henry Regnery Co., 1967) p. 134.

[2] Annie Besant, *Four Great Religions* (Chicago, Ill.: The Theosophical Press, 1897), pp. 18-19.

[3] Manly P. Hall, *Freemasonry of the Ancient Egyptians* (Los Angeles, Calif.: The Philosophical Research Society, 1952), Introduction.

[4] Manly P. Hall, *Twelve World Teachers* (Los Angeles, Calif.: The Philosophers Press, 1937), pp. 20-24.

[5] Dastur Framroze A. Bode, "Zarathushtra's Unique Spiritual Philosophy of Self-Unfoldment," *The American Theosophist,* October 1971, pp. 309-310.

[6] Besant, *op. cit.,* p. 65.

[7] Hall, *op. cit., Twelve World Teachers,* pp. 58-59.

[8] Alvin Boyd Kuhn, *The Lost Light* (New York, N.Y.: Columbia University, 1940) p. 47.

[9] Annie Besant, *Super-Human Men* (London: Theosophical Publishing Society, 1913) p. 19.

Chapter 3

GRADED SPIRITUAL INTELLIGENCES

Various religions of the world share a common belief in a graded development of consciousness. Various cultures express it in various ways, but behind the forms of speech used are similar concepts. Although man, at his present stage of development, does not see the whole plan of evolution, universal changes of potential into powers are evident.[1] Such changes usually involve a long series of graded steps, whether it is in the development of superhuman powers, superhuman men, ordinary men, the angelic hosts, or the lesser kingdoms of consciousness.

The recent concentration of research by some of the world's greatest astronomers upon radio stars and quasars, using enormous directional antennae, indicates the quest for other forms of intelligence in the universe and an interest in receiving signals from extraterrestrial civilizations.[2] If we could make ourselves known on other planets by laser beams or mathematical signals, or by discovering and fixing intergalactic wave lengths, which now seems possible, men might send radio messages throughout space.

The tremendous cost of space exploration makes the search for life on other planets seem futile to some people. They usually do not recognize the 4000 by-products of this research now enriching our lives by being used in hospitals and many other areas.[3] Interest in parapsychology has been increased by such demonstrations as the *Nautilus* experiment in August, 1959, in which a submarine dived hundreds of feet below the surface where radio transmission ceased yet where mental communication between two people functioned. Many other controlled experiments that have recorded mental communication faster than light, are contributing to new branches of exploration. Many of our leading scientists[4] are attempting impartial research to find out if there is extraterrestrial life. All over the world exobiologists are working to break down barriers of thought and to examine ideas which have so long been overlooked and discarded. NASA has a research program outlining eight different probes which might give evidence of unknown forms of life in the cosmos.[5]

The ancient wisdom teaches that there are seven basic forces in nature. In terms of men, there are seven kinds of matter or gradations of substance which form seven planes of existence: the physical (the most dense), emotional, mental, intuitional, spiritual-will, and two beyond (of even finer density) which are to be developed by future evolution. These seven planes, or systems of energy, each with its seven sub-planes, all interpenetrate each other. The form-world is made of those planes in which the form predominates over force and rhythm. The formless planes of the world are the three higher planes of the mental, intuitional, and spiritual-will; in these the life force and rhythm predominate.

Many religions of the world have recognized seven divisions of men and angels in different states of consciousness. They have used different terms, as will be seen, to describe the graded ladder of the various "Sons of God."

Hindu Concepts of Graded Intelligences

The variety of beliefs in India fulfills men's varied needs. Their rituals and ceremonies bring even the more ignorant into harmony with the visible and the invisible in their environment. They are taught through knowledge of nature and inner life that all life forms are interdependent, and they are taught to contribute their share toward the harmonious working of the various intelligences in the different worlds. By giving service to the mineral, vegetable, animal, and human in the physical world, by giving service to the devas or "shining ones" and to elementals in the mental and astral world, and by dedicating themselves to the Higher Ones in the spiritual world, they build a reciprocal harmony in their own life.

Below the one God, Brahman, and its three great Aspects, personified as Brahma, Vishnu, and Shiva, are the seven great "elements." A mighty intelligence rules over each of the elements—akasha, fire, air, water, and earth. (The other two are not yet manifesting.) Lords of Spiritual Intelligence are rulers of each particular element and the life in it.

Below the seven rulers are the many ranks of devas (angels), descending from the great to the smaller form-building elementals. These devas are not to be thought of as having human form but rather as centers of radiant energy surrounded by streamers of force. They do not function in a physical body but in a form more subtle, usually called an astral body. Devas evolve from relatively undeveloped consciousness as found in elementals, form-building energies, and nature spirits but range to the more exalted ones ensouling planets and universes.

A contemporary writer, Geoffrey Hodson, explains that devas and form-building energies exist in the superphysical worlds but interpenetrate and build in the dense, physical substance. He indicates that they are directed by thought and word power to play along lines of force, stimulating and amplifying them to vibrate and to produce form.[6]

Hinduism recognizes in each of these, from the smallest to the greatest (for each is a fragment of God), a conscious entity and subtle form, so that the worshiper may choose from a range his definite object of veneration. As his understanding increases, his object of devotion may be enlarged. His idea of God is in proportion to his understanding. Shri Krishna taught: "Even devotees of other Gods, who worship full of faith, they also worship Me. . . ."[7] The Hindu, whether learned or ignorant, is aware of the range of spiritual intelligences which, in various ways, benefit him. In addition to his duty to cooperate harmoniously with these invisible forces, to which many names are given, he also has a duty to his family and to society.

On the human plane of evolution, the complete unfolding and perfecting of innate divine powers is a long, long journey. The "perfected" man or adept is one who has developed the will to omnipotence, the wisdom for omnipresence, and the intellect for omniscience. He has therefore reached the place where he works in harmony with the plan of Deity.

To conceive of the nature of those who have become superhuman men is beyond the average man's understanding. We know only the little they have thought wise to share with us. Many a man with pure, receptive, and open mind has had glimpses of these powers. Those whose extrasensory perception is developed have given us some detailed descriptions of these great ones. There are many grades of unfoldment, each offering its definite achievement and opportunity to serve humanity.

The training necessary to develop such advanced abilities extends over many lives. Those with great strength, purity, and persistence can shorten the evolutionary process. The two safe ways recommended are by meditation and by unselfish service. At a certain stage of achievement, other instruction is given individually and orally.

The teaching speaks of two "fires." The one is formless, an invisible "fire" concealed in the central "Spiritual Sun" and spoken of metaphysically as triple. The second "fire" of the manifested cosmos is septenary in the universe and solar system. All these are "Sons of Fire" in the universal mystery. The Pitris are Hindu

Lunar Deities and are said to have created physical man. The Seven Kumaras or Builders are Solar Deities and are "fashioners of the inner man."

The "Primordial" are the highest beings in the scale of manifesting existence. They are the archangels in Christian terminology. The Primordial proceed from the "Father-Mother" principle whereas the Seven Builders proceed from the "Mother" who is "overshadowed" by Spirit, not impregnated by Spirit, in the universal mystery.[8] Such an "overshadowed being" is aided during a vast period of growth so that those potentials of the One Essence within are gradually manifested.

Higher intelligences aid the younger ones to evolve by sacrificing themselves for that purpose. Such are the Seven Kumaras, said by some writers to have been the egos who incarnated through the animal men toward the end of the third major stage of evolution. They refused to create bodies until the egos had evolved forms and equipment suitable to receive a mind and to use thought, thus becoming truly human. The Kumaras, by the process of physical embodiment, were deprived of their conscious wisdom so their sacrifice to serve man included the long difficult task of learning to control an animal type body. They were "overshadowed" and guided so that their advanced type became the poet sages who later organized the scriptural writings of mankind.

Since the beginning of self-conscious life, a hierarchy of adepts and initiated priest philosophers taught humanity to cleanse the body, to overcome limitations, and to reunite with his own divine nature.[9] As man's body form becomes more sensitive and finely attuned and as his consciousness evolves toward more perfect awareness and expression, he ascends in the great hierarchy.

Buddhist Concepts of Graded Intelligences

Buddhists teach that religion can be accepted literally and be acknowledged as an allegiance, or it can be experienced mystically at a much deeper level. In the Southern School this deeper dedication requires monastic discipline and responsibility. In the Northern School, the Mahayana system acknowledges that anyone may seek identity with truth in order to better serve mankind and thus modify consciousness and gain a high degree of enlightenment. Buddhists so dedicated are usually teachers without wealth or luxury. A few disciples usually gather around them to learn of their wisdom, humility and composure.

A Buddhist may attain a natural expansion of inner realization and an enlarged degree of wisdom and enlightenment, and then he is called an arhat or adept. His abilities may seem to be miracles to his pupils, but usually what appears wonderful is actually the natural result of law fulfilling itself.

Each man grows by his own efforts. As his abilities and sensitivities increase he may reach a new level of awareness and consciousness. He then has added responsibilities for aiding mankind. Even the most humble person may perform good works and find greater wisdom. There are many levels of attainment, from prehuman to humble human beginnings to exalted beings, forming a vast expanse of development.

The basis of the Buddhist hierarchy is a search for truth but the degrees of realization of truth vary greatly. Buddhist literature makes references to human Buddhas and "celestial" Buddhas.[10] This recognition of a vast hierarchy in levels of consciousness is found in Buddhism as in many other religions.

Egyptian Hermetic Concepts of Graded Intelligences

The Egyptians did not consider their deities as actual persons but as representations of the energies of nature, of matter, of mind and they arranged these intangible powers in a graded hierarchy. They used poetic names for these energies, but their gods did not have human flesh. The intangible powers were given imagined form, but it was the creative energy within the form that was venerated, not the form itself.[11] They had much knowledge of the forces of nature, such as rays, some of which our scientists still explore.

Hermes Trismegistus taught that the Universal One first emanated superior beings which were said to circulate the "heavenly fire which is the life of all things."[12] These Gods were represented by the planets and stars. The Seven Planetary Governors ruled terrestrial life. The orbits of the seven planets (known to the ancients) formed a ladder connecting heaven and earth. Each of the Governors was said to give man one of his own qualities, so man gained seven natures as gifts of the Gods. These gifts are available to man but by his choices he makes himself capable of receiving them.

Persian Zoroastrian Concepts of Graded Intelligences

Records of antiquity are verified by occult students in ways quite different from those used by historians and archeologists. The Great Brotherhood who guide the unfoldment of humanity is said to have preserved the ancient writings in underground temples and libraries where no injury could come to them. Some of these manuscripts, it has been stated, are in the ancient sacerdotal language in which they were written.

A second way occult scholars may verify ancient happenings is by developing ability to read the "Akashic Records." The akasha itself is a subtle medium in which is recorded in the finest detail every event that has happened through the ages. Those who have undergone the discipline requisite for developing the needed sensitivity are able to "see" past events moving before their eyes with living accuracy. Some can "tune in" and search any event they desire to investigate.

Studies of the ancient Persians, attained through viewing the Akashic Records, indicate that the first great

Prophet Zoroaster, like the Hindu Manu, belonged to the same mighty Brotherhood. Zoroaster taught that the universe comes from Divine Intelligence. All living is the Cosmic Fire, the light of intelligence and pure emotion, glowing from within. Different degrees of attainment are achieved from the internal universal process in which all forms naturally unfold. The various stages of evolution are different levels of cosmic intelligence. Any evil or limitation only indicates lack of development, for the heightened intuitive consciousness eventually leads the Higher Self, through self effort, to union with the infinite Source.

Zoroaster guided the early Persians appropriately for their particular needs. The agricultural people were given training that was a combination of philosophy, religion, and astronomical science. The planets and stars represented spiritual intelligences who guided and stabilized the universe and whose will was the guiding law. Astronomy portrayed the spiritual wisdom which was expressed in the material world. The spiritual beings, in all forms of life, ranged higher and higher toward God. Adoration of God and of those intelligences whose forms were the planets and stars fill the fragments we have of their writings. Out of this teaching came the Zoroastrian influence that brought such an expression of divine purity, even to this present time.

Greek Orphic Concepts of Graded Intelligences

Almost every religion describes the descent of the angels or the minor gods in prehistoric times. Much literature was based upon the theme that the angels from heaven descended to help develop the higher animals and to form man. These builders, from high divinity down to man and below him, are the "gods" of ancient mythology.

The Greek Orphic systems described the "river of vivification" in which "the gods" distributed divinity according to capacity, pouring out their life for lower beings according to their receptivity. In Plato's *Timaeus,* twelve legions of "junior gods," sparks of the eternal Flame of cosmic mind, descended to earth to lift the race of higher animals by uniting them with their own form and mental capacities, thus "to weave together mortal and immortal natures."

Only a fragment of God was bestowed when the intelligence of God was joined to the life of an animal: the remainder of the spiritual force remained hidden. The Greeks called this invisible part the "daimon." Modern man calls it the "collective unconscious." It remains and guides man. The divine intelligences which the Greeks called "daimons" were subjected to cyclic incarnation as was man. They therefore served both their own and the animal interests by linking the spiritual nucleus with a material organism.

Religion is more than mystical feeling, piety, and devotion. Its high cosmic mission is designed to transform animal man into divine man. Its rites are made to make man aware of his divine essence, to help him become fully human. Religion is a psychic instrument designed to foster evolution. It instructs the sages so that they might guide man to evolutionary security, step by step. Successive levels of attainment, achieved as consciousness and form evolve, are basic to the whole Greek system. The dialogue of the *Parmenides* gives all the genera in order from the first cause.

The Greek theories of color and music were indicated in the tetractys, a figure of ten dots arranged in triangular form. The uppermost three dots (triangle) symbolized the threefold White Light containing the potential of all colors. This represented the First Cause from which the universe was established. The remaining seven dots represented the colors of the spectrum or the notes of the musical scale and also were the symbols of the seven active creative powers coming from the First Cause. The seven was divided into two parts: the upper row of three dots represented the spiritual nature of the universe; the lower row of four dots represented the material forms. All together they represented the decade, or ten, through which Pythagoras taught that all things in nature were regenerated.

One of the Greek symbols showed streams of force coming out of the mouth of the Eternal One as the white light separated into the spectrum of seven colors, representing the Seven Creative Lords or Logoi. The planets also were described as the Seven Creative attributes of God. The Lords of the Planets, dwelling in the sun, symbolized the seven powers as one in source and essential in nature. The relationships of planets, colors, and musical notes were similar ways of indicating the essential nature as one, yet the divergence into many forms. The invisible spiritual organisms of each planet, as it revolved, uttered a certain tone according to its magnitude, speed, and distance from the sun. The seven strings on early musical instruments were related both to their correspondences in the human body and to the planets. The Greeks also recognized a correspondence between their planets and the seven vowels. Man's mystical nature was represented by the sum of seven symbolized in the six surfaces of a cube with its mystical point within.

According to their "law of correspondence" the whole universe was interwoven in one Substance, all organs were interacting, all organs vibrating with a frequency or resonance affected each other, and therefore these correspondences provided a key to solving problems.

Pythagoras believed man would eventually reach a state where he would no longer function in a physical body but would ascend to the immortals. He discovered that the seven modes or keys of the Greek system of music influenced emotions and diseases of the nerves, and on that basis he developed an elaborate system of music therapy. Plato likewise thought melody and rhythm could be used to increase love and all noble emotions but also hatred and mean feelings. The Greeks recognized that musical frequencies could make popular taste more sensuous or that they could be used educationally to ennoble the mind and change consciousness.

Christian Concepts of Graded Intelligences

All the various classifications of life are "Sons of God." St. Paul described man as spirit, soul, and body (or as having three different types of density) but all united and one with God.[13] He said, "Know ye not that ye are the temple of God, and that the spirit of God dwelleth in you?"[14] At his baptism Jesus claimed to be the "Son of God" because that was the very nature of man.[15] He said that according to the Jewish scriptures, there was a vast range of capacities, but men and angels by nature are all "Sons of God." Just before his crucifixion Christ prayed that ". . . they all may be one; as thou, Father, art in me, and I in Thee, that they also may be one in us . . . I in them and thou in me, that they may be made perfect in one."[16] St. Paul taught that Christ was to be in the heart of each disciple "until Christ be formed in you."[17] Men are eventually to attain "the measure of the stature of the fullness of Christ"[18] by evolutionary growth.

The Scriptures describe the seven Spirits before the throne of God.[19] In the Roman Catholic Church, the angels who aid man and nature are venerated as were the "lower gods" in the earlier religions. St. Paul described superhuman beings who brought experience to man from those cycles of evolution which preceded the earth's development. He described also the interrelation between God and man as a descending order of intelligences called "thrones, dominions, principalities, and powers."[20] The gradation of angelic rank is also described by John in the Book of Revelations as the "Cloud of Silent Witnesses before the Throne—Seraphim, Cherubim, and Thrones." Both angelic and human gradations of development are recognized by Christians.

Several historical developments have lessened the Christian emphasis on graded stages of evolution. The Westerner has long been exposed to the idea of only one called "Master," rather than the more universal concept common in the East in which the term might apply to anyone who attained that elevated degree of consciousness. The exclusive idea of being the "chosen children of God" (fostered by the Church Fathers) eliminated much of the idea of personal responsibility for evolving consciousness. The universal idea that a man's spiritual development toward perfection is based upon his own right action and responsibility for the various degrees of achievement has not been emphasized. The literal interpretation of the life of Jesus as personal history has changed the inner symbolism depicted by the events in his life, so that the universal meaning has been lost.

There are two predominant concepts concerning the birth of Jesus: the orthodox church and sects accept the account in the Bible literally and believe in the immaculate conception; the esoteric and occult groups maintain that Jesus was born naturally but that at a certain stage in his development (baptism) he received the Logos into his own spirit and the Christ Spirit ensouled him. Many think of the Christ as a glorious being guiding evolution and using the human body of Jesus for three years. Thereafter Jesus became one of the Masters of Wisdom and has since guided Christianity and all acts of devotion.

Another viewpoint stresses the Christ of the solar myths, which represent the Logos by a hero on earth. This hero is born at the winter solstice, dies at the spring equinox, conquers death, then rises to the highest heavens.[21] All solar heroes sacrifice their lives for mankind. This sun myth was a universal pattern frequently repeated in ancient literature depicting the greater one sacrificing to aid the lesser ones.

Those who respond to the viewpoint of the Mystic Christ accept the descent of the Logos into matter, calling it symbolically the "birth of the Christ" or the "birth of the Sun God." The sacrifice and limitation in a physical embodiment is called the "cross of matter." It is a voluntary sacrifice the Great One made to bring all the separative forces in man again into the unity of spirit. Those who respond to the mystic viewpoint of Christ understand Annie Besant's words:

> For the Christs of the world are those Peace-centers into which pour all warring forces, to be changed within them and then poured out as forces that work for harmony. . . . There is no substitution of Him for them, but the taking of their lives into His, and the pouring of His life into theirs. For having risen to the plane of unity, He is able to share all He has gained, to give all He has won.[22]
>
> . . . . identity of nature was mistaken for a personal substitution." [vicarious atonement, so they had Jesus taking the place of sinners]. . . . He is one with all His brethren, not by a vicarious substitution, but by the unity of a common life.[23]

Most people find that the formality of a ritual or a picture of the Master aids to visualize and to experience their higher aspirations more clearly. Most people need a definite object on which to focus their veneration. Others attain the same state without such help. The union of the individual self with the universal Self is the process sought. Only this attainment within oneself, only this attainment of spiritual oneness, is true reality.

The belief in reincarnation and karma was currently accepted at the time of Jesus, as our Scriptures indicate in such passages as Matthew 17:10-12; 16:13; 11:14; John 9:2-3; Revelations 13:10; etc. Several centuries after Christ, a Council of the Church Fathers condemned as heresy the belief in pre-existence which implies reincarnation and karma. After that it was necessary to invent vicarious atonement instead of man reaping the reward of his own deeds. The significant law of sacrifice underlies the idea of the vicarious atonement, but it was misconstrued when an innocent one could be punished for someone else, to make justice. No one can redeem another by shedding innocent blood for him. Each must learn his own lessons and accept his own responsibilities. Each develops at his own rate of achievement.

Methods for the spiritual development of man have persisted, and traces of the ancient use of invisible powers in ritual by sound, gesture, and thought are still practiced, especially in the Catholic Church. But until recently, a large part of the Bible's instruction concerning man's possible development toward full humanness has been minimized because the allegorical meanings were not understood. Christianity is a comparatively young religion, and the challenge it offers to man concerning his spiritual development may become more prominent as time passes. Especially it is becoming apparent that man may choose, by his own acts, a slow development or a more rapid evolution. His culture, his religion, his race, his beliefs, may be different or similar to those about him, but it is his evolutionary progress, his growth in consciousness, which is important.

REFERENCES

[1] Geoffrey Hodson, *The Kingdom of the Gods* (Madras, India: The Theosophical Publishing House, 1952), p. 7.

[2] Erich Von Duniken, *Chariots of the Gods* (New York, N.Y.: G. P. Putnam's Sons, 1969) pp. 153-155.

[3] *Ibid.,* p. 133.

[4] *Ibid.,* p. 163.

[5] *Ibid.,* pp. 164-165.

[6] Hodson, *op. cit.,* p. 22.

[7] Annie Besant, *Translation of the Bhagavad Gita* (London: Theosophical Publishing Society, 1916) IX, 23.

[8] E. Preston and C. Humphreys, *An Abridgement of the Secret Doctrine* (London: The Theosophical Publishing House, 1966) pp. 45-46.

[9] Manly P. Hall, *The Adepts — The Light of the Vedas* (Los Angeles, Calif.: The Philosophical Research Society, 1952) p. 51.

[10] E. Preston and C. Humphreys, *op. cit.*, p. 55.

[11] Alvin Boyd Kuhn, *The Lost Light* (New York, N.Y.: Columbia University, 1940) p. 77.

[12] Manly P. Hall, *Twelve World Teachers* (Los Angeles, Calif.: The Philosophers Press, 1937) p. 39.

[13] I Thess. 5:23.

[14] I Cor. 3:16.

[15] John 10:34-38.

[16] John 17:21-23.

[17] Gal. 4:19.

[18] Eph. 4:13.

[19] Rev. 4:5.

[20] Col. 1:16-17.

[21] Annie Besant, *Esoteric Christianity* (Madras, India: The Theosophical Publishing House, 1946) p. 108.

[22] *Ibid.*, p. 154.

[23] *Ibid.*, p. 156.

Chapter 4

CHANGES IN EARTH AND THE UNSEEN WORLDS

There are three or four major conditions or systems functioning simultaneously within human beings. Different descriptive perceptions and methods have given names to classify these states. Scientists also indicate that the atomic nucleus functions simultaneously in the gravitational, electromagnetic, nuclear fields and perhaps in others yet to be defined.[1] New methods in photography are proving that man and other forms of life function at the same time in various states.

The occultist has explored systems and described characteristics with considerable detail. Semantic differences in terms should not confuse the basic understanding that there are various states functioning simultaneously. Most occult students accept that man lives in three or more worlds at the same time. Usually man is not aware that an emotional or astral world, less dense than the material world he sees, interpenetrates his physical world; that mental and spiritual worlds of still finer substance, also interpenetrate the physical and emotional worlds. He lives, simultaneously, in a physical body, an emotional body, and a mental body. He is a living intelligence, a spiritual being, who according to his ability to contact these triple worlds develops equipment which brings him gradually into conscious awareness of them. He materializes the qualities of his consciousness while his bodies are himself externalized.

Spiritual forces evolve in him from the still higher spiritual worlds, from the immutable oneness, to purify his lower bodies and to illumine his consciousness at the three lower stages. This occult teaching is being accepted more and more by thinking people.

Dr. Harold S. Burr, Professor Emeritus of Neuroanatomy of Yale University has shown that all living forms, from seeds to man's body, are electrodynamic fields and are surrounded by such fields. These can be precisely measured. They form a matrix or mold which controls the growth and repair of the physical form.[2] Dr. Leonard J. Ravitz, Jr., also of Yale, has shown the relationship between the human mind and its electrodynamic field. The voltage-gradients vary about an individual, in periods of low efficiency, and may be used to predict the physical and emotional pattern that will follow.[3]

It is indicated that every molecule of the body is molded by the vital energy pattern called by some the etheric energy.[4] An "electrical current flowing along a nerve automatically induces a magnetic field around the nerve pathway." This magnetic field can be precisely recorded by the use of the Delawarr Camera, whose critical rotational positioning increases the luminescence.[5]

The Kirlian type of photography using high frequency fields has enabled Russian scientists to study the plasmic states of the organism of humans, plants, and animals. They have also recorded the effect of color changing the activity in specific oscillations of the "bio-plasma," the effect of cosmic occurrences such as solar flares, phases of the moon, the effect of changes at times of crisis such as accident or death, changes under anesthetics, trance, coma, and ill health. This type of photography has made it possible to see at least part of the aura or energy body which occultists have long described as the vital or etheric, astral, or mental body. This type of scientific exploration is bound to indicate we are more intricately interrelated with the cosmos than scientists had formerly realized.[6]

The Kirlians have found living things have a totally different structural detail than nonliving things with the physical body mirroring the energy body. This energy matrix in all living things, although invisible to ordinary vision, was shown to be a unified body giving off its own electromagnetic field.[7] The Russians call this energy body the "Biological Plasmic Body."

Dr. N. van Dorp van Vliet, a member of the New York Academy of Science, the Institute of Nuclear Energy, University of Stuttgart, the London Institute of Nuclear Engineers and Professor of the Nederlandes Biologische Stichting, Holland, is working on pre-physical energy materialization using micro-magnetic frequencies with amplitudes emitted from audio-sonic magnetic instruments and specimens of mineral salts and other organic substances. These experiments have given pre-physical forms differing in crystalline contours depending on the frequency patterns transmitted. He is continuing his researches in Holland on the formative forces of a nonmaterial state in the universe.[8]

Some have attempted to gain consciousness in the more subtle worlds by using pseudo-techniques, thus injuring their physical brains. Fragments only of the ancient science of the East are published. If any so-called "teacher" tells of physical means by which to unfold consciousness, beware of results. Drugs, physical exercises, or other practices might start a little astral consciousness in the lowest parts of the astral world yet not give larger awareness. Such efforts might force a person into the astral world in an astral body unorganized for receiving impressions or understandings, and at the same time they could make physical life useless by injuring a part of the brain that would be needed later for normal development in the physical world.

Man's intuition tells him this physical world is only the threshold to a larger experience. Many try to force the physical body to reawaken primitive powers of psychism to enter the invisible worlds. What the novice does not usually realize is the vast range of psychic development. The lower states may be either glamorous or horrible but in either case are of little worth; they may lead to tremendous waste or extreme danger. Psychics usually develop only physical capacities, not mastery through the mind.

When a medium leaves his body during trance or sleep, he drifts around in the subtle world and is vaguely conscious of his surroundings but is no wiser if he speaks. Inducing a state of trance by numbing the brain does not make the medium wiser than when awake in the physical world. Mediumship development is a physical state and not a spiritual development. The moral platitudes given are not moral strength; craving for phenomena is not at the level of religious devotion. Frequently the medium has little discernment in selecting who shall enter and take over his body. When the average medium leaves his body he is not actively awake but in an untrained dream state.

There are many more weak and vicious discarnate entities hovering near earth wishing to enter a medium than well developed entities. The more evolved have challenging responsibilities in the higher worlds and do not cling to the earth. It is confusing that an entity returning is called a "spirit." He is, of course, no more spiritual than when he was in the physical world. All men are spirits in some state of evolution.

At present psychism is a fad, but although some lower forms of psychism are common, the sincere searcher needs to know the great difference between the lower psychism (largely linked with emotionalism) and the higher use of psychic powers (used with knowledge and control).

The subtle worlds can only be known by turning attention away from the physical world. This insensitiveness is produced in trance by inhibiting the physical senses and stopping the function of the brain. This can be done by mesmeric passes, drugs, rapid spinning, and other means. Staring at a crystal ball or a white spot on a black background is common. This reduces the brain to partial paralysis or trance and stimulates the feeling center connected with the eye, thus increasing emotion. Decreasing winking causes the retinal cells of the eye to have great fatigue. As the optic nerve is deadened and the brain dulled fragmented stimuli, formerly experienced, may be rearranged ("visions appear").

Breathing exercises whose purpose is to still thoughts by holding breath are often suggested. While the breath is held the blood continues to circulate and accumulate carbon dioxide, thus stupefying the brain. Then certain currents may be directed to enliven obsolete sympathetic nerve centers which become psychic channels. These may be activated but not controlled and may cause great discomfort and harm.

The use of artificial conditions of intoxication and the use of narcotics is a sign of decadence and not of strength. The only safe methods for unfolding consciousness are regular, steady meditation combined with purity of thought, purity of desire, and purity of physical life. These disciplines develop the mind and instruments through which consciousness registers. Pure thought develops the mental body, pure desires develop the astral body, and the physical body must be pure so that astral and mental forces can flow usefully. He who uses chemicals or other means to force open brain centers without psychical control abuses brain-level capacity and may suffer dangerous abnormal effects. One's goal should be to help others, not to satisfy curiosity.

He who uses well the capacities he already possesses, who by his life demonstrates his worth in service, is eventually entrusted with conscious control in the invisible worlds. Capacity is earned by courage, perseverance, right action, and meditation. A tremendous responsibility accompanies its use, in discriminating between lower psychism and higher psychic uses.

Flashes of vision or vivid thought hint that man is greater than he seems, that he is part of a vaster world which surrounds him. Usually he does not think of himself as living on a physical planet within subtler worlds which permeate his bodies, the earth, the universe and the many forms of intelligence. Yet he will become conscious of these invisible worlds when he has learned to still his mind and focus consciousness at other than physical levels.

Occultists believe that during sleep the physical body and brain become almost unconscious except for the automatic, instinctive functioning, when most of consciousness is apart from the physical body in the vast unseen worlds, in an astral body or a body of subtler frequencies. Sleep is restful because the consciousness is away from the physical body and therefore not building up nerve fatigue.

Many meaningless images float through the brain during sleep but some people are able at awakening to recall experiences while away from the body. These memories are quite different from the usual confused dream. They are the beginning of linking the brain and waking consciousness with the consciousness of the subtler worlds.

We are linked both in sleep and in waking states with the invisible worlds. Each person continually receives telepathic impressions from individuals; from the thought of the masses; from those who are living; and from those who are no longer physically present. We are mediums transmitting telepathically according to our sensitivities. Our "thoughts," so-called, may come from books, radio, friends, discarnate beings, from the physical world, the emotional world, the mental world, or spiritual world. Our responsibility is to discriminate and choose to dwell at the higher rather than at the lower levels of these psychic influences.

Stilling the activity of the mind while remaining in full control is a much higher attainment than stilling the mind by fatigue, paralysis, or trance. It is not considered dangerous to leave the physical body to permit a spiritual entity to use it, but it is exceedingly dangerous for a lesser being to enter one's physical equipment because the residue of pollution both physical and psychic might be extremely great.

Birth is entry from the invisible world into a physical body; death is casting away a worn-out body to re-enter the subtle world. In so-called death and sleep we are freed from the limitation of the physical body and our consciousness expands with new experiences. It is natural, as soon as we accept the concept of an invisible world surrounding this one, that we perceive with our senses, to want further experience in it at a conscious level. It is as dangerous prematurely to awaken rudimentary psychic sensitivities as it is for the uninformed to play with explosives. Many money-making books have been printed and many schools formed giving dangerous half-truths. As a result hundreds of lives have been wrecked.

Seventeenth century scientists recognized cosmogony (the theory of the creation and organization of the world and universe) in its modern form, and their "nebular hypothesis" was popular for almost a century before it was temporarily invalidated by new knowledge and theories. Some twenty other hypotheses have been studied. Kuiper's "Theory of Accretion," generally accepted since 1950, is similar to the "aggregation and accumulation" explanation given by H. P. Blavatsky to occult students in 1888. When scientists discovered x-rays, radiations from uranium and radium, and alpha and beta rays, they recognized the "solid atom" as a force-field; the concept of "solid physical matter" changed to illusion; the new concept studies matter as "an accumulation of invisible forces."

Bacteria-like structures have been found in fossils which are now believed to be at least three billion years old. These organisms drew nourishment from compounds in fermentative metabolism, at great depths in water, shielded from ultra-violet radiation. It is estimated that it took another billion years for a biological revolution to develop a self-nourishing respiratory or oxidizing condition.[9]

Man is relatively an infant in the habitation of the biosphere. The changes in chemical make-up of the atmosphere may yet demand further drastic biological revolutions. Scientists are studying the circulation of atmosphere and the varying balance of incoming solar short-wave radiation and the outgoing terrestrial long-wave radiations. Man's intervention in these vast energy processes needs to be studied.[10]

Scientists continue to search for a fusion fuel power which does not require the burning of the world's oxygen supply or hydrocarbon resources, and which does not release carbondioxide combustion products. Quite in contrast is the use of nuclear fission for power, with its waste elements, which are highly radio-active.[11] Man's knowledge and technology bring changes to the world. His greed and his desire to bring quick change might easily retard evolutionary progress in a vast time span.

Scientific theory estimates the mineral structure of the earth to be 4,000 to 5,000 million years old, and life on this planet to be from 2,000 to 3,000 million years old. Man is said to have started independent evolution about 20 million years ago.[12] Similar to some of these scientific findings were estimates recorded in ancient Eastern literature and published in the West in 1888 by H. P. Blavatsky. Changes in the earth and the unseen worlds continually need further study.

Hindu and Buddhist Ideas of Changes in Earth and the Unseen Worlds

The ancient wisdom teaches that living spirit comes into denser and denser forms, shaping instruments in which it can function in both the seen and unseen worlds.

A man living in a physical body can develop bodies in the three lower worlds. The average man's equipment is largely in a dormant state. His higher capacities are latent because his vehicles for perception in the astral world and mental world are so little developed. With meditation and right action, man has the capacity to develop conscious awareness in these worlds and also in the spiritual world. His spiritual body is said to endure through the whole period of the individual's evolution, passing through birth after birth. The spiritual individual accumulates the essence of each earth-life experience which is recorded permanently in his spiritual body as the individual becomes more and more organized. The higher spiritual beings do not usually function in the physical world although they can occupy a physical body if needed.

Modern scientific views concerning the universe are still hypothetical. The "Steady State Theory," studied about 1950, may be replaced by the theories of an "oscillating universe" in which an estimated 80,000 million years makes a complete cycle of expansion and contraction.[13] This current scientific view approaches the ancient Hindu view of cyclic laws basic in the universe, in the earth, and in man himself.

Hindu cosmology recognizes the unmanifested power as underlying all manifested appearances and as making apparent the interrelation in all life and all form. The ancient ones picturesquely described vast concepts of time in the "Nights and Days of Brahma," thus summing up their concept of the cyclic expansion and contraction of the whole universe. "The Great Breath" of Brahma expressed the outbreathing or expansion phase; the inbreathing expressed the contracting phase in the universe and all in it. These vast periods of activity and rest, called "manvantara" and "pralaya," indicate alternating periods of evolution and involution or re-absorption. This is somewhat similar to the current scientific theory of an "oscillating universe," with its present vast expansion phase.

The Hindu idea of cosmic space describes it in the form of a "Great Egg." Recent scientific cosmogony speaks of the curvature of space. The Hindu "World Egg" rests during a "Great Age of Brahma" then breaks open into two parts. The upper hemisphere is golden, the celestial expanse of the skies; the lower part is silver, the mundane expanse. From this Egg were formed the continents, seas, planets, gods, mankind, and all of life.[14] The "World Egg" symbol suggests the infinite in a circle without beginning or end; it suggests the cosmos emerging from endless space. If we accept the interpretation of the World Egg as a cosmic circle, as space, without beginning or end, we approach the identity of deity within the universe and the fact that the smallest particle has an essence of the whole, thus perceiving God not as an outside force, but rather as the unfolding of the laws of nature.[15]

The Hindu concept presents evolution as proceeding in two directions. The form side is developing, as Western science verifies, from the simple to the complex. At the same time the spiritual, psychic, and intellectual side is developing from the highest to the lowest as the spiritual assumes control over the lower levels of consciousness.[16] This dual evolution within the cycle has, of course, not been recognized by scientists. The scientific emphasis, still on the development of form, teaches that life forms evolve step by step through the various minerals, plants, insects, amphibia, and animals, but the theory has gaps and "missing links" about mind and man.

Hindu concept states that when the form reached high enough development in the animal structure, the germ of mind was given by great beings from more advanced "planets." That which distinguished man from animals is this "gift of mind," given directly from spiritual sources. Mental capacity, according to the Hindu teaching, did not evolve through the animal, as Darwin and others have implied. The human stage manifests through a long series of births and deaths during which spirit evolves.

In Hindu symbolic geography, universal energies and forces are personified. The idea of the world mountain is described in the *Vishnu Purana* as the abode of the Gods, located on the earth's oldest outcropping of rock in a remote sanctuary. From this center embryonic humanity was vitalized until enough spiritual wisdom unfolded to produce men or those able to contact the source of eternal life. The *Puranas* also outline the consecutive history of the world, destined to take place on seven "continents." (The terms "continents" and "moon planets" as used in the *Puranas* are not identical with modern usage.)

There is a modern scientific theory that all continents were once joined in one land mass called "Pangaea" which dispersed into ten major plates with continents resting on them. The continents are thought to have drifted thousands of kilometers during a few million years to their present location.[17] The ancient teaching of "continents" said to exist previous to our present format (Lemuria, Atlantis, etc.) may be only symbols of events in the subtle worlds. Mankind has gone through several marked stages of development which extend over vast periods. Through each, desire-motivated energy has impelled expression. When these desires dominate excessively, they become as a great flood of the ocean or a great fire and destroy civilization. When the desire-motivated thoughts are controlled with the certainty of a unitary formative power, consciousness and form develop harmoniously toward a link with the higher Self. Argument about the existence of such continents only detours our mental and emotional energies away from the significance of a steady growth toward essential values.

In *The Secret Doctrine*, by H. P. Blavatsky, written

in 1888, the ageless wisdom from many sources indicates seven schemes of simultaneous evolution in our solar system, each ruled by a great being or Logos. Chains of being were linked together in their evolution. Our world, in its cyclic sequences, is now thought to be in the fourth chain of one of a series of seven. Little is known of the first and second, but we are told that the "moon planet" belonged to the past third chain and that it is now disintegrating because it has served its purpose.

Each major evolutionary stage of mankind develops on its own land formation, during seven vast epochs. The first two "continents" fostered pre-human life in its embryonic forms as the senses of hearing and touch were developing. In the third vast epoch, sight was developed on the continent called "Lemuria." It stretched along what is now the Pacific Ocean area, the southern part extending to Australia and New Zealand. Easter Island and Madagascar were mountain tops of this "continent." The seven Kumara Solar Deities were sent to give Lemurians the mental equipment which distinguished man from animal. After this long process, in which both land forms and man reached higher states, the continent of Lemuria vanished. Great waves rolled over it, and volcanic explosions and fires tore it to pieces. Only a few remnants of land remained, and only a relatively few people survived.

A fourth "continent," called "Atlantis," appeared between what is now Europe and America. It also existed for a tremendous span of time, and was the home of the fourth evolutionary stage in which the sense of taste was developed by the same monads evolving birth after birth. Seven distinct civilizations evolved in this fourth evolutionary stage as people intermarried and made new combinations of types. Finally this "continent" too, having served its purpose, was broken into parts and almost totally submerged. The people who survived later intermingled with other tribes and formed the fifth developmental stage in which the sense of smell was developed.[18] Great swamps in Europe and Hindustan slowly dried some 60,000 years B.C. to form the land occupied by the nucleus of the fifth group. A few families had been safely led to the area now known as the Gobi Desert region.

The ancient writings further state that a future "continent" would rise out of the Pacific Ocean and be the home of the sixth human stage of development. Earthquakes, volcanic eruptions causing tidal waves and floods might be expected to come eventually, but they would be spread at intervals of thousands of years. The seismic changes would destroy local areas but would never destroy the whole human race. While new land areas would gradually form, the consciousness of the new evolutionary stage would also develop.

The Hindu writings make clear that catastrophies are means of progress. The world at certain times becomes exhausted and needs to be renewed in order to carry forward the evolutionary plan. In the course of time, the plan indicates that a still more highly developmental stage of the same monads would inhabit yet a "seventh continent." Hindu cosmology compresses into a single plan the repetition of enormous cosmic changes on different planes of manifestation.

Egyptian Ideas of Changes in Earth and the Unseen Worlds

Hermes Trismegistus taught that "the vice of the soul is ignorance, the virtue of a soul is knowledge. . . ." The usual modern attitude classifies the ancient beliefs as superstitions, but the ancient scholars' writings refute this. Their central idea, restated in many ways, is that the lower physical natural or brute forces are to be controlled by perfect harmony and balance, and that training the reasoning intellect is a divine art. Their philosophy taught that true evolutionary development is to be attained by uniting the forces of spirit with those of the world; thus the lower is to be disciplined by the higher. They encouraged the individual to advance by cultivating wise habits in his daily living, teaching that an inner principle of consistency fosters in life a continuing process of becoming. This gives man a sense of stability and usefulness. The idea of process was succinctly expressed in the *Book of the Dead,* by the soul "steppeth onward through eternity . . ." in one life after another. Spirit was accepted as reality, the mundane world as less real.

The Hermetic teachings, upon which many early Egyptian and Mediterranean beliefs are based, taught that great "celestial fields" were known in the unseen world and later were established in terrestrial geography. The real world is the heavenly world, the home of the gods. The earth is the underworld, called "Amenta," the place of illusion and death. Much of their teaching has been misinterpreted because they symbolically represented earth life as dead or unreal.

Many tales in Egyptian and Greek mythology represent the solar hero as descending into some place of darkness where he suffers, conquers physical nature, and emerges victorious, having attained higher spiritual values. Many versions teach the same concept. Racial experience is also described by means of stories with the same general theme. The Biblical Israelites, wandering in the wilderness and in Egypt, symbolize a people groping to gain spiritual experience. The term "Egypt" is often used, not as a place on earth, but as a symbol to indicate a state of illusion or a period of difficulty.

Such terms as wilderness, desert, cave, cavern, abyss, and pit refer to human psychological struggles. The god descends into the cave or darkness of the human body, suffering through the earthly underworld, but rises again to the light of the higher spiritual worlds. In the tale of Hercules, the soul tracks the lion (symbol of the Spiritual Sun) into the cave to capture it. The Egyptian Horus awakens "the sleepers in their caves."

In the *Ritual,* Ra is said to enter the cave to "revive the heart of him whose heart is motionless." The soul which dwelt in the cave or secret dwelling-place of the body was called forth by Jesus on several occasions.

The universal solar myth told of the god or hero descending from a higher state to suffer in the dark region of the unknown world until, conquering the illusions of the lower world, he rose again to the promised land of the spiritual world. The earthly body of man was the Egyptian's theological world of darkness. Into this world of darkness the Spiritual Sun brought light in order to transform the lower world into the higher world, to synthesize all divided natures into the original unity.

Symbolic Egyptian astrology depicted mankind's birth in the zodiac in the house of the Virgin Mother, Virgo. The sun, symbol of Spiritual Fire, descended into the western darkness of the physical underworld and rose again in the East, symbolic of regenerated spiritual man. A body in which such a transformation took place was often likened to a city, the City of the Sun, called "A-NU" by the Egyptians and "Heliopolis" by the Greeks. Much later Egyptians built the earthly Egyptian city of A-NU, where the priests presented an annual drama portraying Osiris or Horus in the rituals of death, burial, and resurrection. Nature supplied much subject matter that the teachers identified by analogy and used to impart exalted spiritual understandings; thus they helped their pupils to comprehend intuitively the concepts of universal order and unity. Egyptians did not worship material things, nor did they write much about changes in the physical earth.

Symbolic astrology expressed ancient religious wisdom. The soul's experience was believed to be depicted in the chart of the heavens, and spiritual history on a cosmic scale was thought to be portrayed in the heavens before man was born on earth. The history of the human soul, first written in the starry skies, was extended in various forms before it was written in literary scriptures. Alvin Kuhn describes the Somerset zodiac in England, calculated to have been built 2700 B.C., as covering one hundred square miles. (To suggest its size, the distance from nose to tail of Leo, the Lion, was four miles.)

The Heavenly Man, whose bodily cells and organs were the sun and the planets, was the prototype for man. The divine Cosmic Man became the secret anatomical graph, and early man was taught to make all life "after the pattern in the skies."

This general "pattern of things in the heavens" was so widely accepted that events and places came to be described in symbolic terms. The literature from various cultures is thus not yet truly understood. Celestial typology was grafted onto topography, and over long periods of time spiritual concepts were recorded as a nation's history. Kings and heroes were part of the heavenly drama that prevailed in many lands. The names and events of assumed history made up much of the early literature that has been so confusing to Western habits of thought.

Back of all racial, national, and human history the ancient religious teachers indicated the pattern in the skies. The scriptures and the epics were fashioned to simulate the structural unity in the divine plan of the cosmos and man. Typically, according to Kuhn, one finds the holy city, or the center where rulers and leaders lived; the Upper and Lower Land were heaven and earth, or spirit and body. A river, to describe the union of the divine and animal principle, connected the higher mountainous kingdom with the lower kingdom, bringing fertility and the living water to the lower area. The typical history also included a neighboring sea (symbolizing the emotional turmoil of mortal life) and a lesser body of water crossed by the soul to reach bliss. Land was divided into seven provinces to typify the seven stages of unfoldment or the seven kingdoms of nature.[19]

The seer sought everywhere on earth for archetypal design. Only the wise ones in the mystery schools understood this concealed universal wisdom; only those capable of rightly using the power were entrusted with deeper knowledge. Only in recent years have scientists begun to measure the gravitational pull from the movements of sun, moon, and planets in the cells of man and other smaller forms of life. It is now recognized that "the influence of space penetrate everywhere."[20]

Zoroastrian Ideas of Changes in Earth and the Unseen Worlds

The formation of the cosmos from the viewpoint of Zoroastrianism is known only from fragmentary remains. Early writers said that "Time" by its progression rejoined its Source. Iranian calculations of the duration of the world varied. Some said a cycle of 12,000 years or "Limited Time" was created by Ormazd. "Unlimited Time" preceded and followed the limited time period. In other words, their concepts of history were not eternal because they regarded "Time" as more inclusive than the manifested creation. A catastrophe of fire or water would end history, thus permitting a new birth of the world. Boundless Duration or "Zravane Akarne" would reappear in cycles of activity and rest.

Ahura Mazda, the "Germ" of Creative Power, was the "Force of the Motion proceeding from the Primal Source." The glory of Ahura Mazda was too exalted for human intellect and the light too resplendent for human eyes. This incomprehensible primordial principle, the central Spiritual Sun, was a hidden force. During its active period it sent forth creative light or radiant energy, manifesting both man and cosmos. The first of Ahura Mazda's creations were the Sky of the Universe and the Light of the World. Out of Ahura Mazda evolved divine ideas, fire, and sound.

Zarathushtra taught that there were six periods in the evolution of the world. First the canopy of heaven was formed; the steamy moisture of the clouds precipitated the water; the cosmic atoms consolidated into earth; vegetation developed; animal life evolved; mind took form in man; and the seventh period, yet to come, promised the Persian Messiah. After that the solar system would be extinguished for a period of rest.

One ancient authority mentioned thirty-three kinds of "land," but it described only seven. The central one was physical consciousness, with other "lands" around it on the East, West, Southeast, Southwest, Northeast, and Northwest. These descriptions in the *Avesta* were not locations on earth; they provided a descriptive diagram of the chain of development in seven parts. The seven parts, in turn, manifested in three different planes of consciousness.[21]

The "melody of the aether," mentioned in the *Oracles of Zoroaster,* was the "current of the life-wave" from the One Life;[22] this root-sound (the akasha), then became air, fire, water, and earth, thus evolving the universe. The Great Power continued involution and evolution through vast cycles. A very old book described four Zoroastrian ages with four races of men: the Black, the Russet, the Yellow, and the White. In man were centered all the forces, both visible and potential. The inner, immortal man was that Ego which incarnated in physical form, but the Ego existed before its physical body was born and survived its physical body because it was the spiritual counterpart of God. The "celestial doubles," or Divine Ideations, were first formed as spiritual prototypes, both of the universe and of man.

The common archaic concept included a center where heaven and earth met. Serving as a link between physical earth and higher globes this center, sometimes called "White Island," could not be destroyed. Their teaching described it as presided over and protected by the three sons or rays of Zarathushtra. This idea was similar to the Greek Mount Olympus and the Hindu Mount Meru which represented a condition of consciousness known as the "abode of the gods," not physical locations.

According to Iranian cosmology each terrestrial phenomenon, both concrete and abstract, corresponded to its invisible celestial center. For instance, in Mesopotamia, the Tigris River had its invisible model in the star Anumit, and the Euphrates had its model in the star of the Swallow. The temple particularly was a sacred place that duplicated a celestial prototype. Its celestial plan was said to have been revealed in a dream to the architect because its archetype existed as a model in the region of eternity before terrestrial architecture began.

It is said that a map of the entire region about the sacred city of Babylon was first revealed, surrounded with vast fields that were bordered by a river. Later the city was built. Bible references describe the celestial city of Jerusalem which existed before the actual city was built. Cities, rivers, mountains, and sanctuaries had an extraterrestrial archetype which was the plan of the form or the celestial "double." ("Archetype" as used in this sense by the ancients is not the same as the term used by C. G. Jung in relation to the "Collective Unconscious.") If there were no separation between man and his archetype, or the celestial center or pattern in the sky, there could be no individually separated mind; all were related in the one pattern of the total Mind. Modern man tends, instead, to think of himself as an individual center around which he imagines a world as a limit. Man will find peace only as he achieves a concept of space without an individual center and boundary about it: "There is no 'individual' mind at all—we are all totally related."[23]

Modern scientists have examined moon rocks and established that the moon is much older than the earth. In the early writings of the *Avesta,* the Parsis addressed the moon as "Mah Gao-chithra," which means "the Moon that bears in it the seed of earthly life." It was believed that the Lunar Monads incarnated on the earth for higher evolution, and that because the purpose of the moon had been fulfilled it began to disintegrate.[24]

Orphic and Greek Ideas of Changes in Earth and the Unseen Worlds

The ancient system of cosmology used terms such as "earth" and "world" to mean invisible superphysical spheres which are the archetypes of the earth and world as man knows them. Plato's teachings, based upon the wisdom of the ancient Orphic and other traditions, described the perfect unity from which all diversity is suspended; a basic pattern is repeated throughout creation's infinite variety. Each individual is a product of unity, each item is a unity in its own nature, and from each is suspended another chain of diversity—on and on indefinitely. The physical universe is the mortal body of an Immortal Divinity. Mankind is a degree of spiritual activity within the consciousness of God.

The Pythagorean doctrine taught the relationship of lesser "wholes" to greater unities. Man is similar in pattern to the universe, and as a microcosm he is a miniature of the World Macrocosm. The Universal Creator, according to Pythagoras, fashioned two types of bodies in His own image: the cosmos, made of sun, moons, and planets, and man. He taught that even man's internal parts reflected the universal pattern.

Some writers have stated that the placing of the human figure in sanctuaries did not represent idolatry but was only a symbol to remind man of the harmonies and proportions of the world. A pattern of the human species in its most perfect form was used to measure, by estimation, the proportions of the world and the cosmos. Measurements of symbolic man were basic standards used to measure and estimate the proportions of the universe.

Anatomy and physiology were studied in order to learn divine knowledge.

Orphic theology tells of the radiant energy buried in the flesh of the body, with the said organism "suspended" from indestructible Fire. Heraclitus described the relationship between body and spirit as a "portion of Cosmic Fire, imprisoned in a body of earth and water."[25] The link between body and spirit was "more ancient than the body," inasmuch as the soul and the consciousness had experience in one incarnation after another, gathering wisdom as its harvest.

To the wise men of old, the names of the four elements—earth, water, air, and fire—had profound symbolic meaning. These wise men did not teach that all material things were compounded of these four elements; rather they taught that the original Essence had compounded and formed four distinct modifications or planes of nature: the physical (symbolized by earth), the emotional or astral (by water), the mental (by air), and the spiritual (by fire).

The pattern, repeated in man, endows man with four "bodies," each finer one interpenetrating its coarser neighbor. The division between them is not spatial, but rather in the form of potency. (Their "harmonizing" might be compared to the matching of frequencies when one "tunes in" on a television station.) To step from one body to another necessitates raising the "frequency of consciousness," or as the wise men have expressed it, by "harmonizing with it."

One wonders what kind of bio-energy Dr. Robert Pavlita in Czechoslovakia is transferring from living bodies to nonliving matter by means of his psychotronic generators. The bio-energy, at first, was focused by a subject's staring in patterned sequence, thus charging a generator and also changing the sender's biological field. Now the vital energy from any living thing (plants, animals, humans) is said to collect due to the position of specific materials in relation to the form of the generator.[26] Modern technology is opening new areas of knowledge about interpenetrating energies which may be changed to other dimensions.

In *Timaeus* Plato spoke of the Chaldean idea of the Great Year which would end when all the planets met, causing a universal upheaval. He was also familiar with the Iranian idea that such catastrophies were to change and to purify the world and its people. The popular motif of the eternal return and the end of this world period to make way for a new type of world in which people would be freed from old age, death, and decomposition and would be reborn was consoling to people who suffered from disease, aging, and poverty. This archaic concept recurs over and over in old literature—in Homer, in Hesiod, in Chinese writings, in the Old Testament, and in many other records. Its challenge is not generally accepted as the immutable whole with the vast cyclic patterns in all nature.

Hebraic-Christian Ideas of Changes in Earth and the Unseen Worlds

Those of the Christian faith who consider the physical body a temporary possession of the spirit for only one short life span need hardly trouble to develop it. Some have even neglected and belittled its significance. Others, reacting to the concept of a worthless material body, have sacrificed everything to its pleasures and have made bodily sensations of greatest importance in living.

The physical body might well be considered a valuable possession and be guarded as such because it is the form through which we function and through which higher degrees of consciousness may register. To make it a fitting instrument of spiritual forces, we ought to nurture it carefully and sanctify it as a holy possession. We need to make it pure by keeping it clean, by abstaining from toxic materials, and by protecting it from evnironmental disorder. It is an instrument that we are privileged to use.

Today many people accept the fact that emotions and thoughts affect physical conditions. Also, growing numbers of thinking people are accepting the possibility that levels of consciousness are functioning in vehicles or systems more subtle than visible material substance. Acknowledgment of both of these concepts can improve the mental, emotional, and physical states of the individual through his recognition that each person needs balanced conditions to best serve his spiritual purposes.

The ancient ones taught that the life force stored in the hidden depths of the earth is sufficient for man's needs. The outer surface of the earth would be tilled until exhausted and would be polluted in many ways, but it would be broken up by readjusting forces such as wars, storms, floods, upheavals, and cataclysms. Then, from below the hard crust, new energies would be released which are suitable for advancing more purified forms of life; the life giving properties of vegetables, fruits, nuts, and grains would be disease-resistant and disease-preventive.

It is time that man awaken to his depletion of the earth. Chemical poisons in the air, the waters, and the earth speak of man's ruthless greed and thoughtless use of natural resources. Clearing of forests, which formerly gave off oxygen, and the building of roads where formerly moisture was stored, have radically changed the conditions of the earth and the environment. The ancient teachers recognized that selfish enmity, inharmony, impurity, and destructive thought forces would accumulate in the astral world and would be precipitated upon the earth in the forms of insects, plagues, and disease; and man has indeed perverted and wasted his resources and his creative powers.

Modern youth questions, "Unless the whole round of life and all its activities make sense, why live?" They are perplexed by present standards of value which seem superficial and without purpose. Science has taught that every action brings an equal reaction, that every cause sets up its effects. Frequently this concept has not seemed pertinent in our daily living, where a short life span indicates no permanent realities. Our culture has stressed one physical life span as its whole, rather than as part of a long evolution in consciousness and form. Yet, just as one's idea has expanded from one's community to international and now to interspatial views, so too many people are groping for a logical expanding view in the development of consciousness and form.

There is challenge in thinking of an ascending series of development from mineral to man along "a horizontal dimension of time" combined with a descending evolution of subtle powers which give rise to higher types of existence. The ancient teaching that a dimensionless flame of consciousness unites with the spatial properties of a matrix to form the first stages of atoms and electrons whirling in a web of energy, emphasizes an inner order of precedence apparently before solidity of form. Such a reoccurring order of subtle formative powers gathering outwardness of form about themselves may be applied challengingly at every level of manifestation.

The concept that form and consciousness evolve, cycle after cycle in a spiral of development and refinement, indicates a logical understanding of the many forms in the earth and in humanity. The great range also in the unseen parts of the world, in the differences in consciousness of simple life expressions and the complex man stage and the much more advanced stage of the adept, indicate a continuing progression.

In modern times men are replacing ideas of a personal God with concepts of universal awareness. Their old limited idea of God is passing into a clearer realization in depth. It is good to bring to the surface ideas long hidden in the heart (whether by tradition or by early indoctrination) by clearly focusing attention on them in words and form. A man's concept of God may change, not die, as he reaches new levels of understanding. As one realizes man's identity with the Higher Self, he recognizes there is one potential in all the unfolding forms of life. He may have to cut back his early conditioning to the basic structure of being, like pruning a tree, in order to grow again in fuller realizations. When man begins to work consciously upon himself, he is using a different process from the one he uses mentally in studying about philosophies, religions, history, and peoples. Beyond the mental, in the subconscious and superconscious parts of his nature, he who seeks will reach new levels of understanding.

In our racial childhood, symbols typified ideas and feelings, but we left these behind for a while as we explored the material world. Now humanity is turning again to read the glyphs and pictorial ideograms of the past, to synthesize understandings, to gain psychic wholeness and control, and to gain alignment with divine purpose. The Christian God-idea has guided man through centuries, from tribal rule to a democratic concept in which the individual is responsible for controlling his baser instincts and working for the common good. Valid understandings of eternal values are replacing dogmatic beliefs, thus avoiding chaos and disillusionment. As consciousness develops self-directed awareness, the individual learns, through personal effort, to surmount the causes which deter his progress and to use disciplines which hasten his development.

It is unfortunate that Christian theology did not perpetuate the pagan concept of the pulsating, vibrant universe which modern science is exploring. Instead it perpetuated the Jewish Old Testament background as explaining the origin of the universe; the New Testament teaching lacked cosmological and anthropological background.

Modern physics is bringing focus upon our world with

renewed insight. For several centuries physicists emphasized exploration of separate objects, detailing the surfaces, boundaries, and unique characteristics of each structure. The new physics now emerging implies that all entities and all systems are part of a total time-space continuum, although some of them function in different states or conditions. Modern field-theory physics describes our world as part of a larger pattern, as a subsystem within a larger conceptual whole. Each part or entity is observed as related to other parts in continuously expanding fields. Instead of emphasizing structure, much exploration now focuses upon functioning relationships.

The atom is now understood to have a center surrounded by invisible forces; many consider the wave theory as valid a system as the particle theory; and man's consciousness is coming to be recognized not only as a center for individual use but also as a purposeful part of a much larger whole. Universal challenge and personal responsibility dawn gradually upon the individual as his understanding expands. Man's concept of the earth and the unseen worlds is continually revised. Form and consciousness continue to change. Galaxies, solar systems, atoms, and particles each seem separate and perishable, but the real universe is now recognized as nonmaterial and continuous.

REFERENCES

[1] F. L. Kunz, "The Reality of the Non-Material," *Main Currents in Modern Thought,* 20:39, Dec. 1963.

[2] H. S. Burr and F. Northrop, "The Electro-Dynamic Theory of Life," *Main Currents in Modern Thought,* Vol. 19, Oct. Nov. 1962.

[3] L. Ravitz, "Periodic Changes in Electromagnetic Fields," *Annals of the New York Academy of Science,* LCVIII, 1960, 1181.

[4] George de la Warr, *News Letter Radionic Centre Organization,* Oxford, England: Spring 1968 pp. 2-3.

[5] G. de la Warr and D. Baker, *Biomagnetics, A Study of Finer Forces of Nature,* Delawarr Laboratories, 1966, Oxford, England.

[6] Sheila Ostrander and Lynn Schroeder, *Psychic Discoveries Behind the Iron Curtain,* (Englewood Cliffs, N.J.: Prentice Hall Inc. 1970) p. 215.

[7] *Ibid.,* p. 213.

[8] N. van Drop van Vliet, "Crystallisation of Radionic Frequencies," 1969 *Newsletter Radionic Centre Organization,* Oxford, England: winter.

[9] Evelyn Hutchinson, "The Biosphere," *Scientific American,* Sept. 1970, Vol. 233 No. 3, pp. 52-53.

[10] Abraham H. Cort, "The Energy Cycle of the Earth," *Scientific American,* Sept. 1970, p. 54.

[11] Gough, W. C., and Eastlund, B. J., "The Prospect of Fusion Power," *Scientific American,* Feb., 1971 Vol. 224 No. 2, pp. 61-62.

[12] Jean Raymond, "The Evolutionary Cycles and Their Chronology," *The American Theosophist,* 57:142-143, May 1969.

[13] Hugh Murdoch, "The Nights and Days of Brahma," *The American Theosophist,* 57:126, May 1969.

[14] Manly P. Hall, *Man the Great Symbol of the Mysteries,* (Los Angeles, Calif.: The Philosophers Press, 1937), p. 115.

[15] Murdoch, *op. cit.,* p. 130.

[16] H. P. Blavatsky, *The Secret Doctrine,* An Abridgement by E. Preston and C. Humphreys, (London: Theosophical Publishing House, 1966), p. 169.

[17] Robert Dietz and John C. Holden, "The Breakup of Pangaea" *Scientific American,* Oct 1970, p. 30.

[18] Geoffrey A. Barborka, "The Concept of Brotherhood and Root Races," *The American Theosophist,* 58:40, Feb. 1970.

[19] Alvin Boyd Kuhn, *The Lost Light* (New York, N.Y.: Columbia University, 1940), pp. 80-81.

[20] Michel Gauquelin, *The Cosmic Clocks,* (Henry Regnery Co., Chicago, Ill.: 1967), pp. 143-144.

[21] Nasarvanji F. Bilimoria, *Zoroastrianism in Light of Theosophy,* (Bombay, India: Theosophical Publishing Society), p. 129.

[22] *Ibid.,* p. 85.

[23] J. Krishnamurti, *Talks in Europe 1965,* (Ojai, Calif.: Krishnamurti Writings Inc., 1965) p. 71.

[24] Bilimoria, *op. cit.,* p. 88.

[25] Kuhn, *op. cit.,* p. 41.

[26] Z. Rejdak and Korel Drbal, "On the Third Form of Energy," *Periskop,* (Prague) Czechoslovakia, 1967.

[27] S. Ostrander and L. Schroeder, *op. cit.,* pp. 258-359.

Chapter 5

UNIVERSAL LAW

Modern scientists work within laws of physics as they explore both seen and unseen worlds. They have explored in physical and superphysical fields, but in no way in supernatural fields; yet they have extended our knowledge of nature beyond the tangible physical world. Metaphysicists, by contrast, are predominantly speculative. Science has finally brought us beyond sensed knowledge to the nonmaterial, natural, but provable knowledge, and has verified some of the metaphysicists' hypotheses. No longer, in many instances, need we rely on belief, for modern science now proves much that formerly had to be accepted on faith.

For example, we no longer think of matter as occupying empty space. Force potentials within and without each atom, object, form of life, and process unite and integrate them into one universal process. The atoms and molecules form localized actualities (or "illusions") to our physical senses, but the universal space potential in the force field is the underlying reality. Physicists work with the laws governing the continuum behind both material substances and nonmaterial energies; everything that happens takes place within the laws of the space potential universe.

The universe is a cosmic expression of that which human faculties cannot know or totally describe. The principle of Oneness transcends our capacity for comprehension; we can know it only by what it becomes. Because we are infinitesimal parts of the One Principle, we are necessarily expressing and developing portions of that Oneness which comes out of Itself. The process of becoming is the essence for us. The self-actualizing process overcomes the limitations of the lower self and gradually becomes the higher Self. We need to recognize the mind-entity in the totality of being and becoming.

The Absolute One, in order to be known, had to become two, and the new relationship became the third manifestation of the Absolute One as It applied life to form.[1] The One remains, yet develops into many life forms which much later merge again with the One. The process involves coming into being in a life form, then ceasing to be by merging again with the One; or it may be described as an impersonal life force whose harmony is broken and then restored, or whose perfect equilibrium between the swing of opposite actions is continuously restored. This ebb and flow, everywhere present, moves as small cycles within larger cycles throughout the universe. The law of cyclic development is a universal law that applies to solar systems and galaxies. Tiny life forms and biological materials also undergo these cyclic changes in order to continue.[2]

The basic cyclic law as it works in human evolution includes the law of action and reaction, a law that automatically works from cause to effect, producing unerring justice. The universal harmony is changed by each person's acts, by each thought and each word, by each event, and by each circumstance. Every change sets up a sequence of adjustments that modify related circumstances, and the sequence continues until the adjustments finally restore the original harmony. The disturber of harmony is himself responsible for the disturbance, and the law of adjustment immutably follows until the cycle is fulfilled and the disturber has learned a lesson from his experience.

One who accepts the idea of the Whole, and himself as a part of the Whole, accepts his limitation within the Whole; he accepts the law of the whole process which gives him his own freedom within that limitation. He recognizes the sequence from the Source of "Be-ness," through the process of "Becoming," to the goal of "Being."

In order to find the All from which we come, we need to search, as completely as possible, within the All of the universe and within the All of ourselves. We cannot hope to understand if we seek only with our minds, or seek only with our emotions, or seek only with our perceptions. In our study of cosmology we attempt to understand both the invisible and the visible, and to discern the direction of events and their interrelated harmonies as they apply to mankind. The battle which began in the nineteenth century between science and religion gradually lessens as we use a nontheistic approach to problems of human betterment and evolution.[3]

We can most quickly attain growing awareness of the essential Oneness (call it identity with Deity, or discovering the Self, or by any other name) through compassion, sacrifice, and suffering. This, of course, the Eastern seers have taught for ages, whereas the Western wise ones have sought external knowledge. Now these two approaches are coming closer together as we begin to recognize that philosophical knowledge and practical working are parts of one whole, as we bring into focus both power and the awareness by which we perceive, and as we identify the Self of man with the Oneness of the universe. We can never achieve this merging, of course, until we leave the complexities of the intellect behind and dare to enter the subconscious part and the superconscious part of our being. Only then do we begin to change ourselves instead of rationalizing about our need to change.

Some Areas of Exploration

Much interesting work is being explored in various scientific areas which will ultimately speed up knowledge of subconscious and superconscious capacities. Julian

Huxley has said that all living substance has mindlike properties usually far below levels of detection.[4] This has been proven by Cleve Backster's lie detector apparatus which has shown plants' responses to threats of being burned and to other destructive thoughts or to helpful thoughts.[5] Also, he has recorded much evidence showing "primary perception" inherent in many other types of living things.[6]

A great deal of work is being done by top level engineers, physicists, physiologists, biologists, and geologists in Russia and elsewhere to investigate capacities beyond normal brain functioning. Dr. Ippolit Kogan reports many successful experiments in guiding a person by telepathy,[7] a capacity which could have use in war or peace.

The vast amount of work done under the leadership of Dr. Georgi Lozanov in the Institute of Suggestology and Parapsychology at Sofia, Bulgaria, is utilizing much knowledge gained from ancient Eastern wisdom, combined with modern psychiatry and medicine. Dr. Lozanov has shown that thought can increase healing, control blood flow, and anesthetize the body without the use of drugs and their adverse after-effects. The combination of Eastern wisdom and Western knowledge opens vast new areas of usefulness.[8]

The Czechs, employing the most modern scientific instruments, are researching to find more about "psychotronic energy" (auras), reincarnation, healing, alchemy, and other areas of latent powers.[9]

Dr. Davidovich Kirlian and his wife Valentina, working in Russia with high frequency generators and electronic microscopes, showed the change in the aura as a leaf withered and died. They presented differences in the aura in two seemingly identical leaves from the same species of plant, one of which had been contaminated with a serious plant disease and which soon died. Photographs of the leaves indicate diagnostic possibilities.[10] The pattern of luminescence differed for each item, whether living or inanimate, showing continuous change. The Kirlian photography shows that an energy flows from the human body, radiating a healing or destructive effect on itself, or on plants or the environment; it indicates a transfer of energy from the "bioplasmic" body of a healer to the "bioplasmic" body of the patient.[11] If a leaf is cut, the part which has been removed still registers the energy pattern of the whole leaf (the "ghost").[12]

The research for twenty-five years at the Delawarr Laboratories in Oxford, England, into the ecology of living cells in the human body has indicated the potential use of magnetism in lowering cholesterol in the blood and in reducing the white cell count—useful discoveries for the treatment of cardiac diseases and leukemia respectively.[13] Frontiers open with these many forms of exploration which use new instruments to give proven insight into laws universally applicable to the formative processes in all nature.[14]

Hindu Concepts of Universal Law

The ancient Hindus believed that a Divine Will operates through a master pattern and that all creation expresses that pattern. The universe unfolds by an infinite succession or repetition of this basic pattern on different levels or planes. All bodies, races, institutions, and worlds are different forms expressing one essential nature. All structures reveal a master law governing the universe.

Hindu cosmology teaches that besides the visible universe of effects is the invisible universe of mind and cause. The attributes of the Supreme Being form a hierarchy that rules over this great scheme and that works through the various levels of creation, generating, forming different manifestations, and teaching.

The Manu incarnates as the quality of the Divine Mind, directing the evolutionary development in man's spiritual, intellectual, and physical energies. This Manu, or life-mind principle, provides the vital impulse which brings the major stages of unfoldment into existence, which promotes the ethical principles that preserve mankind, and which contains the mental potential that develops and guides the people.

The laws of Manu, according to Hindu teachings, are revealed as a guide for man's development both collectively and individually. They are not just for the people of India. Vaivasvata Manu, the name of the present Manu, typifies the collective plan for the present stages of mankind's unfoldment. This evolution continues in vast time spans through religions, philosophies, sciences, arts, and crafts. The early Hindu civilization had the basic characteristics out of which the Manu Vaivasvata, or the collective guiding intelligence, directs succeeding cultures.

Two codes of ethics are given: a higher secret tradition for the dedicated pupils, and another for the masses. The law governing the dedicated pupils brings them through self mastery to truth. The less exacting law governing the world interprets the teaching on levels of morality and social usefulness and brings the masses to expanded knowledge more gradually. (Originally the caste system was part of this attempt to guide the people but became outmoded.) Both types of law are needed because spiritual knowledge alone cannot fulfill evolutionary needs, and physical knowledge alone cannot unfold truth.

The individual is taught that he must make the choice between the real and the unreal. In the *Bhagavad-Gita,* Krishna instructs Arjuna that the first requirement of true devotion is obedience, and that he must overcome illusion, not blindly reject it, if he is to attain the real. Arjuna will have experiences in the world, but he is not necessarily of the world. He is part of a pattern of laws which hold all beings; these he cannot break without disturbing all others. Each individual must learn and choose for himself—no authority can make decisions for or save another. The eternal conflict between illusion and reality necessitates an individual choice, the price of which will be justly fulfilled by the impersonal law of action and reaction.

Both Hindu and Buddhist teachings describe the universal alternation of opposites moving in a round of cycles within cycles in which the law of karma functions as an all-inclusive law of justice. Action and reaction are ultimately equal; a cause always precedes its effects, to be followed by adjusting effects. The law is neutral and impersonal, but one which each man continually sets in motion with his own thoughts and acts. Those in the East understand this law as an agent building human character through countless ages of incarnation, but they tend to accept it passively, as philosophy. In the East and in the West, when this concept is truly grasped, earnest students will feel driven to do all they can in daily activity to speed their evolution by direct forms of discipline.

Metrical speech, composed of a number of syllables, has certain numerical proportions which may be modified by the way it is intoned, giving different results. These laws were studied by early seers. Each sound is known to awaken corresponding resonance in the invisible world, even as vibratory effects from higher worlds affect man's subtle bodies. A certain word sets up measured vibrations in spiritual force and is known as the sacred word. But words have not the slightest power unless uttered by one who is perfectly free from doubts, who is absorbed completely in the uttered thought, and who has cultivated the purity and will power to project and conquer opposing forces. Such words cannot be translated into another language because that changes the sound vibrations.

The Brahmanic deities are personifications of universal consciousness and mind. Consciousness has many forms but is one in substance. The gods who develop organisms and ensoul them are extensions of divine thought and consciousness. By applying a process of meditation, the Hindu makes mental images and identifies with them, thus giving them form. The Brahmanic scholar assumes an all-pervading law. He divides learning into three segments, the first dealing with man and with all animate and inanimate things, the second dealing with conscious awareness extending from the self to successively developing states culminating in adeptship, and the third dealing with the gods, or consciousness and its creations.

Buddhist Concepts of Universal Law

Buddha was convinced that the immediate and necessary task of each disciple was to reform his own character. He therefore refused to discuss with them the metaphysical questions which might lead to speculation and confusion. He stated principles pertaining to the life of man which are so reasonable and practical that they are still considered significant. Within himself man must earn and experience his enlightenment or "salvation." No outside force can redeem him. The fruits of his own labors tell the merit of his way of life. What is right must produce right, truth must yield truth, the good must give goodness. Buddha did not advocate world revolution to correct suffering or failure in personal lives or in world management, but he advocated individual reform.[15]

War, disease, poverty, death, and the innumerable symptoms which even yet plague man and society indicate that we have not yet recognized that only basic right action can yield right results. We are such creatures of habit that it seems incredible that society's basic ways of thinking could be wrong. Change takes courage, and the masses have neither courage nor perseverance.

Buddha taught that each man must decide whether he will drift with the ignorant crowd or face the responsibility of changing himself and helping the world. A universal law fulfills itself through each one who attains an expansion in realization. The law is not imposed on the disciple, rather the disciple harmonizes himself with its purpose in order to serve. Basic right challenges the human being who is essentially true, dedicated, and devoted to right principles. Each man must decide whether he chooses to follow the traditional pattern and suffer the traditional pains or to follow that which is right. The sincere person would not want to add to the world's collective burden of ignorance. He might even teach his convictions to others as long as he did not try to force his beliefs on them.

Buddha's first sermons gave his disciples the Four Noble Truths about suffering.[16] He explained that no man could gain happiness by an effort of will, but instead he must correct the cause of his unhappiness. With characteristic directness he stated that the basic cause of suffering was being born, not because he was born into a body but because of his sense of selfhood, will, and separateness. He decided that birth and death related more to the development of self-will and I-ness than to bodily development. He observed that the collective pressures in society were extensions of the individual's separative drives. If collective social trends brought ills, the individual's impulses must have been wrong.

Buddha taught that man's excessive willfulness is not consistent with the common good and causes suffering. He becomes aware of his own personality and loses collective awareness. As a separate person he suffers in psychological competition with others. His struggle to dominate robs him of the cohesive concept that all are united and one with universal life. His excessive egoism is also a root of other forms of error, such as insecurity.

Buddha's second Noble Truth pertained to the origin of suffering because of possessiveness. He taught that what we call self is only a collection of perceptions and sensations we have acquired. The self is a summary of what a man knows of truth and mistakes, of reality and nonreality. Man continually tries to impose this complex of knowledge on others, whether it is right or wrong. As long as a man builds his ego and tries to perpetuate it, he will not have moderate drives. Because the mind is part of this ego-complex, the unprejudiced mind reports only the uncertainties of life. The attitude of mind is the significant factor. When possessiveness and personal satisfactions and dissatisfactions are the measure of an individual's purpose, he suffers.

Buddha's third Noble Truth concerning freedom from suffering dealt with the transformation of the individual. Suffering begins in the self and must end in the self. It has nothing to do with the action of others, nor can man escape it or solve it vicariously. Man suffers as a result of his own attitudes toward society and his own selfish desires.

A man may suffer unselfishly, however, from the misfortunes of others, as in self-forgetting service to humanity. Compassion is the nearest to selflessness and the least attached to the ego. The instincts of possession, domination, and ambition, which accompany selfness, are the pressures which cause personal struggles and internal conflicts. Only by surmounting all desires except that for right thoughts and action can a man achieve freedom from suffering. If man loves one thing above others he is incapable of the wisdom of the middle way between joy and sorrow. Only if he releases the limits of self-interest and expands to universal concerns will he overcome suffering.

The fourth Noble Truth is the path which leads to the end of suffering. Suffering is caused, not by man's possessions, but by an intense sense of possessiveness; desire destroys a man's sense of values. Buddha recommended moderation; he taught his disciples to detach their minds from the ever-changing and to seek permanent values. The middle way, seeking control between the opposites of joy and sorrow, love and hate, birth and death, would bring wisdom and immortality.

He taught his pupils to overcome cravings and desires by developing insight, by destroying the delusion of self and dependence on external rites, by controlling the five senses and the mind, by rightly using material things which are for use and not for delight only, by courageously enduring discomfort and pain, by avoiding obvious dangers in companions and places, by removing evil thoughts, and by cultivating higher wisdom.

Buddha warned against certain hindrances: uncontrolled feelings that make emotional disturbances; a closed mind and limited convictions that are detrimental to growth; faulty perceptions that lead to frustrations; ego-consciousness that deprives one of universal relationships; and mistakenly accepting appearances or illusions as realities.

He recommended a middle path, known as the "Noble Eightfold Path," consisting of attitudes to be cultivated by the disciple seeking liberation.[17]

1. Right point of view: the student's motive should be free from selfishness, glamour, and self-emulation.
2. Right aspiration: he should be determined to let the law work through his life.
3. Right speech: he should use words harmlessly.
4. Right action: his daily conduct should express his beliefs.
5. Right mode of life: his daily life should be appropriate to one who is seeking truth.
6. Right effort: all his energies should be directed toward essential purpose; he should serve in harmony with law rather than selfishly.
7. Right recollectedness: the pupil should strive continuously toward the purpose of the doctrine.
8. Right meditation: he should withdraw his energies from involvment in the senses and external interests.

Gradually the disciple should be permeated by the doctrine and approach Nirvana.

A Buddhist disciple tries to live by these concepts which, if made the law of his life, lead inevitably to the state of peace and bliss, or Nirvana.

Buddha was called the "Enlightened One" by the many who came to consult him. Men felt his indescribable wisdom as he counseled the elite and the downtrodden alike. He was described as radiating a halo of light; he was clothed in a yellow robe held with the three strands of spirit, mind, and body tied into one cord of consciousness. He sought permanent realities by avoiding all extremes. He renounced the kingdom of comfort, the gratification of desires which gave only momentary happiness.

Northern Buddhism teaches that one could become an adept without accepting Buddhism and without a teacher to guide one because it is from the light within that man gains wisdom. The disciple improves society by his own internal enlightenment; he serves with his inner powers more than with his outer personality, as he seeks identity with universal law and truth.

Eastern adepts did not become rulers or brilliant scholars or men of wealth and power, but they were known for gentleness and humility. Like Western adepts, they demonstrated so-called miraculous powers; their emphasis was upon the power working through them, not upon a power that they possessed. Interior realization gave a natural expansion so that the Law was fulfilled. The reality within each man was his teacher, not a personality. The sincere student seeking the transcendent life found the truth and universal laws which are not found by deductive reasoning.

Egyptian Hermetic Concepts of Universal Law

The priest-magicians of old Egypt had a profound knowledge of natural laws. They emphasized the visible and invisible constitution of nature; Isis personified Universal Nature, the mother of all and the "Queen of Wisdom." The priests realized that there were many truths beyond physical sense perceptions and that in nature there was a cause for every effect, even though there were many effects whose causes were not understood. Modern science acknowledges cause and effect in physical action, but the Egyptians recognized that basically all causes are superphysical—mental, moral, or psychological. They sought to perceive and classify causes. Their form of learning, based upon long training in the knowledge of subjective life, has not been attained by present cultures.

Those who have belittled the "magic" of the priest-magicians have confused it with sorcery. Most Egyptian priests practiced an exact science based upon nature and its laws. They did not believe in the supernatural any more than do our modern scientists; instead their knowledge and work based on natural laws extended beyond physical sense perceptions. The priests had learned how to ascend from the material state of consciousness to a consciousness of universal purpose. By this means they possessed great power.

The Great Pyramid of Gizeh stands as a record of the knowledge of very ancient peoples in the Nile Valley. The date of its construction is still disputed. Many scholars have spent years of their lives trying to find when it was erected, by whom, and for what reason, but the mystery of antiquity surrounds it still. Some consider that it was not built by a primitive people, and many believe it was built by a culture long before our records.

The Great Pyramid, which covers thirteen acres, is one of the largest structures in the world. The mathematical calculations and relationships found in the structure amaze scholars. Knowledge of the laws of mathematics, engineering, acoustics, astronomy, and profound symbolism make its scientifically accurate structure a fitting symbol of divinity, truly an image of time and eternal existence. The feat of constructing it with simple machines and of lifting huge stones and fitting them so exactly is only a small part of its marvels.

Calculations from its dimensions have enabled modern mathematicians to figure accurately the distance of the sun from earth. Their knowledge of astronomy was utilized by so constructing the descending shaft to the pit that the star Vega shines directly through it. The four sides of the pyramid are in direct line with the four directions, indicating that its foundation was based on the laws of nature, and upon this foundation was built the symbol of the "resurrection of spirit out of matter."[18] It was a symbol of immortality in the pre-Egyptian wisdom, and the temple of the mysteries was the place of light, life, and truth. Recent work by Dr. Robert Pavolita in Czechoslovakia indicates that the pyramid shape forms a resonant cavity with specific qualities of energy. This shape radiates an energy collected by a psychotronic generator which completely baffles electronic scientists.[19]

Temples in all lands were dedicated to the worship of divine powers. They were cleansed of evil; in the world of conflict they were protected and sanctified areas where divine invisible powers, represented by sages and prophets, could focus energies to regulate and aid man's survival.[20]

The Great Pyramid symbolized the gate to eternal life for those who succeeded in passing from the material world into the transcendental parts of nature. During initiation the disciple experienced divine enlightenment; he experienced firsthand the illusion of death (changing consciousness) and the rising again to serve in the world of men. It was this wisdom, developed to a high degree, which brought the wise from all parts of the world to study the laws known in Egypt. The Great Pyramid was like the fabled Mount Olympus, Meru, Sinai, and other high places of God where man found union of himself with the Supreme Deity.

Persian Zoroastrian Concepts of Universal Law

Zoroastrian teachings present the law of the universe as a dual force while working as creative energy, as a unit when at rest. The polarization of centrifugal and centripetal attraction keep the earth revolving, and throughout nature counterbalancing forces are either in conflict or in temporary stability. The Chaldean Kabala taught the secret laws of this war of forces. Step by step the initiate-priest, as his knowledge increased, was taught the secrets of these powers.

After a priest attained a well-ordered life and some degree of purity, he had to be "prepared" by ceremonial purifications. He was not allowed to touch certain objects, not because of physical contamination, but because his magnetic aura might cause psychic defilement. When he became more pure he could improve the subtle invisible radiation in the atmosphere and surroundings. Therefore he was described as retiring to the topmost chamber of the temple or to seclusion in a forest or cave, or on a mountain height where no stranger with impure magnetism could influence the atmosphere. Zarathushtra received the *Avesta* on Mount Ushidarina, Moses was given the tablets of *Law* on Mount Sinai, Mohammed received the *Koran* on Mount Hara.[21]

Occult students from remote times have been aware of possible foul obstructive magnetism from man, animals, plants, and minerals. That is the reason that only those well prepared were permitted to enter the holiest places. It was not exclusiveness but a knowledge of psycho-physical law (a distinct dualism expressing actively the conflicting forces in all nature, and a unity expressing balance or rest).

Each student who prepared for initiation had to learn of these laws of force by direct personal experience. Early Zoroastrianism, like other groups, had two schools, one for the primitive Iranian and another for the more spiritually advanced pupil. The advanced group was taught much about subtle powers available for man's use. They were taught to be aware of interrelated environmental magnetism, and to know that purity of body, thoughts, and emotions influenced their powers of projection. For instance, the priest gathered fire for the altar from many sources because the spiritual source of fire pervaded all nature (the motion in each molecule was life expressed as physical heat). He lighted the fire from one blaze to another to remove defilement until only the purest essence remained. The earliest high initiates had developed purity in body, thought, and deeds, and sufficient will power to draw fire directly to their altar. It was exceedingly dangerous for a man to attempt such uses of universal law until he was highly prepared. The fire was kept ever burning on the altar as a symbol of the inextinguishable spiritual Fire, that boundless, universal life, that hidden Light of Light, Source of all.

These early initiate priests learned many ways to use the subtle polarized energies. They experimented with and knew many laws which have since been lost. They knew that wave motions could be altered and systematized to a degree that would alter physical substance and more subtle substance. For them the reality of the object was not in its outer form but in the inner life that molded it.

Greek Orphic Concepts of Universal Law

The Orphic supreme law was that of harmony and equilibrium. It taught that all forms of consciousness exist in a state of harmony, but that if the harmony is changed to a state of disharmony, all phases affected have to adjust through reaction after reaction until harmony is reestablished. A chain of reaction continually follows each action, from the point where the cause of change starts until the cycle of adjustment brings a new state of balance or harmony. This just, impersonal law continually brings harmony in every portion of life, in the world of matter and in the world of spirit.

Pythagoras demonstrated this relationship with a mathematical foundation worked out in music. He is credited with discovering the diatonic scale, or the ratio of tensions in the strings which produce harmonic intervals. The key to this harmonic theory was hidden in the Pythagorean tetractys, a pyramid of ten dots, said to reveal the mystery of universal forces and processes in nature, or the ratio of intervals in the octave. The "octave" represented any whole unit. Pythagoras not only discerned the relationship in the harmonic intervals of the diatonic scale but the relationship of the intervals and harmonies in the spheres. He searched for laws in the gradations of energy and substance between earth and absolute unconditioned force. The Hindu had called this field of relationship (represented in our senses as sound, acoustics and musical interval) "the akasha."

Pythagoras classified harmonies by mathematical proportions and used mathematics to demonstrate the exact method by which harmony, the Good, and the Beautiful, were established and maintained in the universe. He demonstrated the existence of certain natural laws by dividing the vast number of parts of creation into planes or spheres. Each was assigned a tone, a harmonic interval, a number, a name, a color, and a form. He demonstrated the accuracy of his deductions about correspondences on the different planes of intelligence and substance and their relationship by applying his theories, ranging from the most abstract principles to geometric solids. He applied the law of harmonic intervals to all phenomena in nature.

Pythagoras used the harmonies of stringed instruments to influence the mind and the body, developing an elaborate music therapy; much of this work has been lost. Harmony responded to harmony, and Pythagoras believed that when the frequencies of consciousness were raised high enough, man would recognize the divine melodies, the music of the spheres. He believed that everything that existed had a tone frequency, as modern research has verified.

The relationship between music and form was part of the Greek mysteries. If the mathematical requirements of harmonic interval were realized, the elements combined in any structure (such as a building) were likened to a musical chord. The study of sound and mathematics was closely related. The relationship of numbers was a sacred search; the building of a temple, as in modern Masonry, was studied symbolically.

The Greeks applied harmonic interval also to vision, studying the motion between light and form (the essence of color) .

> . . . nothing is self-existent . . . color, arises out of the eye meeting the appropriate motion, and that what we term the substance of each color is neither the active nor the passive element, but something which passes between them. . .[22]

Geometric figures were used to reveal the mysteries between universal nature and deity:

> The symmetrical solids were regarded by Pythagoras, and by the Greek thinkers after him, as of the greatest importance. To be perfectly symmetrical or regular, a solid must have an equal number of faces meeting at each of its angles, and these faces must be equal regular polygons, i.e., figures whose sides and angles are all equal. Pythagoras, perhaps, may be credited with the great discovery that there are only five such solids.[23]

The symmetrical solids are (a) the tetrahedron, which has four equilateral triangles as faces; (b) the cube, with six squares as faces; (c) the octahedron, with eight equilateral triangles as faces; (d) the dodecahedron, with twelve regular rhombs as faces; and (e) icosahedron, with 20 equilateral triangles as faces.

Modern scientists have difficulty appreciating Pythagorean and Platonic astronomers because they were not concerned with the material arrangement or composition of heavenly bodies. They looked down upon the study of physical astronomy because they considered stars and planets the focal points for Divine Intelligence, and therefore regarded philosophical astronomy the reality. At that time men believed that the earth occupied the center of the solar system, and that the sun and planets moved about the earth. Nevertheless, Pythagoras maintained that a flaming radiance was the real center of the universe, which he called the "Grand Monad."

Much later the Council of the Illuminati drafted a system of cosmology and anthropology based upon earlier findings; for a long period this system was reverenced as the scriptures of mankind. It described the divine plan which was to overshadow the evolution of the cosmos, and it set forth the laws governing both mind and nature. After the third century, when the influence of Plato diminished, the keys to understanding were lost and corruption followed.

The ancient wisdom teaches that evolutionary progress depends upon a trained, reasoning intellect, and upon applying to one's personal life the laws and arts of divine balance and harmony. Man must learn to control the lower physical forces by the disciplined higher forces. The hidden teachings provide a study of how to master the powers and how to work through law and order to achieve advancement.

Hebraic and Christian Concepts of Universal Law

The Hebraic and Christian religions emphasize the basic truths grounded in previous great cultures and religions; but Christianity has added emphasis upon compassion, self-sacrifice, and individual responsibility. It has spread to an estimated 800 million people.[24] The three major forms of Christianity are: The Roman Catholic, the Greek Orthodox, and the Protestant groups.

It is hard to describe the multiple and diversified sects of Christianity brought about by intellectual and emotional separative influences. In 313 A.D., the Church was recognized in Rome as legally equal to other religions; in 380 A.D., the Church became the official religion of the Roman Empire; in 1054, the Eastern Orthodox Church split from the Western Roman Church for organizational reasons; and in the sixteenth century, the Protestant Reformation started the succession of Lutheran, Baptist, Calvinist, and Anglican branches, with hundreds of splinter groups following. These divisions came about mostly because of organizational reasons.

Most of the Christian groups are based upon an historical life of Jesus, a little known carpenter born in Palestine probably about 4 B.C., during the reign of Herod the Great. Although the birthday of Jesus is celebrated now over the entire earth, historically there is no record of his birth. Even a description of his appearance is lacking. He is known by his sayings and his deeds during three years of life spent teaching near his home and doing good to those in need. His healing and helping were never done ostentatiously, never to dominate or amaze people. Nevertheless, society condemned him as a criminal and crucified him.

Was it what Jesus said that brought a new dimension to people's thinking? He put his driving convictions into simple, dynamic idiom; he put spiritual values first; he challenged men to change, and even today men try to deny his teachings. He emphasized God's love for man and man's need to be receptive to this love and to pass it on to fulfill others' needs. His humility and complete self-giving, his tenderness, his absence of hypocrisy, his sense of equality, justice, peace, and joy, all endeared him to his followers. It was not so much the "Golden Rule" or the "Sermon on the Mount" or his ethical teachings which evoked enthusiasm, for all these teachings might have been found in earlier traditions. That which stirred the masses with new hope and awe was the power to rise from the dead, the challenge of a constant resurrection of the spirit entombed in the physical universe.

The enthusiastic reports of his disciples and their radiant joy and increased power was not based upon a material biological resurrection but upon a spiritual resurrection: "Christ in you, the hope of glory." This consciousness was attained by loving service for others. It was a challenge of spiritual fortitude to know "I am the resurrection and the life," and to recognize that spirit transcends life on earth. When spiritual awareness triumphs over selfishness and self-indulgence, this potential, innate in each man, enables him to live in a larger dimension, not for self but with compassion and understanding for all mankind.

The Church Fathers emphasized the personal historical life of Jesus and the materialistic physical suffering, death, and resurrection, whereas his immediate disciples (like the more ancient seers) recognized that the pattern-sequence pertained to a state of consciousness, not to a materialistic condition. Bettering one's position appealed to the popular masses but unfortunately obscured the spiritual essence of the scriptures. Even yet the majority of Christian sects emphasize the physical body and personal ambition, still obscuring the spiritual teachings. The Church's early years of competition, of proselytizing, and of persecution and its years of struggle against materialism are passing. Modern science is bringing universal converging concepts into focus.

Nineteenth Century Materialism

Nineteenth century materialism was based upon the hypothesis that matter and energy were the reality of things and beings. A human being was his physical body. The complex universe was thought to have evolved in a time-space continuum from random happenings and with no directional intelligence. Now the scientific view has shifted from seeking the surface appearance to seeking structural form, looking for the total framework or pattern to explain the part.[25] From matter as a system of energy, this may well include a search for subtler systems of matter, coming nearer to the occult search for both physical and superphysical explorations of the universe. Scientific procedures now also use intuitive insight into the unified nature of the universe in order to study the consequences in man's destiny.

When Louis de Brogilies discovered that the electron was not a "particle" but a nonmaterial "wave," a whole new line of thinking started; the universe was no longer regarded as mechanical and predictable. Scientists found that the waves do not move in a tangible "ether." Light exists without being a vibration in "ether." The function of the invisible wave is determined by its frequency. Thermodynamics indicate that each object emits heat. Its intricate vibrational pattern is related to its material substance and its form; each unique object emits a sound, the higher overtones influenced by the atoms of the form and the lower overtones influenced by its shape.[26]

Now that the atom has been proved to be nonmaterial and made of invisible forces moving with incredible speeds about a center, this means that all "solid" things which our senses see and feel are also made of invisible energies moving faster than we have power to observe. The universe and space are one, force potentials are everywhere in the universe, and frequencies permeate all forms and consciousness.

Most people have not yet realized the full impact of these provable facts. The idea of a universal force field of measurable potentials gives some students a more definite answer to man's age-old search to understand cosmology than a statement of belief that a separate "God created" His world. The idea of infinite creative powers, even within the smallest particle, may give a clearer understanding to current problems of race, national groups, and religious separativeness. Astronomers and physicists have now proved that complete isolation is impossible as our world is one interrelated whole. Yet many persons still believe that the earth is the center of the universe and that God's primary concern is with the people on earth. Science has proved facts that replace our former dependence on belief. Minds today demand a law of harmony between belief, thought, and action. Instead of praying to a personal God, asking for forgiveness and for personal favors as the "Grace of God," twentieth century thinkers recognize a universal, immutable law unfolding in all forms of life everywhere. No personal favors are handed out unearned. The laws of nature and the universe proceed with impersonal justice, unfolding a divine harmony.

We are in a confusing transition from a materialistic viewpoint to a clear perception of the universal laws which unite all peoples, races, religions, and cultures as segments which comprise this stage of man's development. It is our privilege to use all of the best contributions that mankind has so far realized. When we understand basic realities we, too, should find unifying harmonies.

New Perceptions of the Twentieth Century

We need to learn the general principles which give direction and which clarify man's place in the universe, his nature, his mode of evolution, his destiny, and his purpose. We need to learn by direct experience to verify truth and reality. We need to learn how to transcend the limitations of language so we may better understand each other. We need to view a whole pattern and then recognize the various relations of the parts of that whole.

Gradually the pattern of man's development is unfolding: he was first worked upon and guided unconsciously; later he was ruled by Divine Kings whom he saw and obeyed; later he was ruled by ideas and directions from unseen sources; and finally he must surmount outside authority, finding the law within himself by which to live in harmony.[27]

A great process or law has been at work down through all the ages as life forms have passed through the various kingdoms of development. Each entity, during the long evolutionary process, added certain capacities as it progressed through the mineral, vegetable, and animal kingdoms to the human level. Each life experience added definite capacities as the entity progressed through many cyclic births and deaths. The first men were crude in body, mind, and spirit; but as these same entities incarnated in one race and culture after another, new experience was added. The old form died in order that a higher might be born. These same entities incarnated in different lands and cultures, having many lives in each racial type. They needed experience in each race and each form of development. Man had to become conscious of the laws around him before he could know the laws within himself.

For ages in Greece, Egypt, Persia, India, and other lands the mystery schools taught that man could surmount the limitations of biological death by changing his level of consciousness. The stories of heroes, demi-gods, and sun-gods were all based upon the theme that man could overcome his animal nature (crucifying it) and rise anew (resurrecting) to a more glorious existence. This same theme is repeated over and over in many forms in the Bible.

Christianity of the future will help man realize that the quality of each form of life is its important factor. Mankind will realize that truth is not found through any particular philosophy or religious system because truth is more inclusive than man's thoughts and institutions. Such material measures as color of skin and place of birth will not be emphasized, but the level of consciousness will be valued. At the unconscious level man has inherited human experience from all ages. We will eventually realize that all are one in the sense of coming from one source, one potential. Christianity's great contribution will be to challenge men to change within, not in order to save the individual self, but to relate the self to all other human beings. This is the law of selfless giving typified by the Christ.

REFERENCES

[1] Christmas Humphreys, "The Pattern and the Law," *The American Theosophist,* 57:103, May 1969.

[2] Evelyn Hutchinson, "The Biosphere," *Scientific American* Sept. 1970, vol. 223 No. 3, p. 50.

[3] Sri Madhava Ashish, "The Secret Doctrine as a Contribution to World Thought," *The American Theosophist,* 57:107, May 1969.

[4] Julian Huxley, *Man in the Modern World* (New York, N.Y.: The New American Library – A Mentor Book, 1960) p. 77.

[5] Bacon Thorn, "The Man Who Reads Nature's Secret Signals," *National Wildlife,* Vol. 7, No. 2, 1969. pp. 6-7.

[6] Backster, Cleve, "Evidence of a Primary Perception in Plant Life," *International Journal of Parapsychology,* Vol. 10, No. 4, 1968.

[7] Ippolit Kogan, "Telepathy, Hypothesis and Observation," translated in *Radio Engineering* Vol. 22, pp. 141-144, New York.

[8] Shiela Ostrander and Lynn Schroeder, *Psychic Discoveries Behind the Iron Curtain* (Englewood Cliffs, N.J.: Prentice Hall, 1970) pp. 275-6.

[9] *Ibid.,* p. 301.

[10] *Ibid.,* p. 191.

[11] *Ibid.,* p. 194.

[12] *Ibid.,* p. 201.

[13] G. W. Delawarr, and D. Baker, "Magnetic Therapy," *Mind and Matter,* Vol. 6, No. 2, Dec. 1966, pp. 2-7.

[14] Lancelot Law Whyte, *The Next Development in Man,* (New York, N.Y.: The New American Library of World Literature, 1962) p. 199.

[15] Manly P. Hall, *Twelve World Teachers* (Los Angeles, California: The Philosophers Press, 1937), p. 101.

[16] Manly P. Hall, *The Noble Eightfold Path* (Los Angeles, California: The Philosophical Research Press, 1937) pp. 24-28.

[17] *Ibid.,* pp. 54-62.

[18] Manly P. Hall, *The Phoenix* (Los Angeles, California: The Philosophical Research Society Press, 1956) p. 164.

[19] Ostrander and Schroeder, *op. cit.,* pp. 357-365.

[20] Manly P. Hall, *The Secret Teachings of All Ages* (Los Angeles, California: The Philosophical Research Society Press, 1945) p. XLII.

[21] Nasarvanji F. Bilimoria, *Zoroastrianism in the Light of Theosophy* (Bombay, India: Theosophical Publishing Society), p. 10.

[22] Hall, *op. cit., Secret Teachings of All Ages,* p. LXXXIV, Citing Plato in "Theaetetus."

[23] *Ibid.,* p. LXVII.

[24] Houston Smith, *The Religions of Man* (New York, N.Y.: Harper and Row, 1964) p. 226.

[25] Ervin Laszlo, "The Recovery of Intuitive Wisdom in Contemporary Science," *Main Currents in Modern Thought,* 25:120, May-June 1969.

[26] Frances Paelian, "The Symphony of Life," *New Age Interpreter,* 29:8-10, No. 4, 1968. Citing Donald Hatch Andrews.

[27] Max Heindel, *Rosicrucian Cosmo-Conception* (Hammond, Indiana: W. B. Conkey Co., 1937) p. 302.

Chapter 6

CONTINUAL UNFOLDMENT OF CONSCIOUSNESS AND FORM

A dual development of consciousness and form is taking place in each kingdom of nature on earth. Physical awareness and hardness are the ideal in the mineral kingdom; sensitivity and beauty of plant form are developing in the vegetable kingdom; self-consciousness in feeling and thought is developing along with form in the animal kingdom; and man slowly develops full humanness and perfects form. "Perfected man," sometimes called an "adept" or "master," has powers in full conscious unity and is in controlled cooperation with universal order.

Consciousness is one's self, the all-inclusive reality. Although consciousness is usually described in triple parts as spirit, soul, and body, it is clearly one. The highest part of our nature, the spirit, might be described as the innate essence or germ of divinity. It develops gradually as it organizes appropriate life forms for instruments of expression. The soul might be defined as a temporary expression in matter of the denser part of spirit, reflecting into the physical body and the world. The physical body is the temporary tool or instrument through which the soul and spirit find expression.

The triple condition in the waking consciousness of everyday activities we know in the dense matter of the brain as our senses, our emotions, and our mind. These faculties work through the limited physical body but only reflect the larger consciousness of the soul and spirit. In other words, consciousness is a unit which expresses in many forms and levels.

The spiritual body is relatively permanent. Many accept that is lasts through the whole development of an individual as he passes through experiences in one life after another. The impermanent dense body and the intermediate body return their elements to the world from which they came, after a brief period of expression. The spiritual body is thought to retain the accumulated memory of experiences gained life after life. The entity lives in his spiritual body, not interrupted by births or deaths, and his consciousness gradually unfolds. The individual starts as a living spirit, coming into denser and denser forms, contacting matter in each of the worlds, and using the substance at each as a purposeful instrument until he achieves mastery. As consciousness unfolds, the form is made of correspondingly higher "frequencies." Every change in consciousness is reflected in a relative change of form for the same atoms are arranged differently.[1]

Consciousness registers in whichever plane one is functioning. We achieve awareness on the astral plane when our brains are developed highly enough to respond to frequencies of the astral plane. When our brain frequencies are developed sufficiently we also register waking consciousness on the mental plane. In the evolution of man, self-consciousness had its earliest beginning in a center in the physical brain. Man, at present, usually identifies himself with this brain center, so in his waking consciousness he is limited to physical awareness.[2]

A root or transcendent essence exists within each form. This subjective center functions in similar patterns even though the outer form may vary greatly in the long evolution from atom to man. Usually much later human consciousness identifies with the universal Self. Man can better understand his development if he recognizes the various levels of consciousness unfolding the individual self into the Self of the universe. He remains at his own level a man, but with Self awareness he eventually identifies with the universal essence.[3]

Each of the world religions includes some kind of training system for those who choose to expand their awareness. Most cultures provide one training for the masses and another much more difficult for a selected few. The steps of attainment for the advanced candidate are usually climaxed with graded tests or "initiations." Since the Dark Ages, the Church has largely discredited these mystery schools so that such instruction had "to go underground."

In the mystery schools the initiation ceremonies were based upon what might be described as a "philosophic death" (leaving the old) and a "psychological rebirth" (ascending to greater awareness). The priests knew a great deal about natural laws and could temporarily aid the higher subtle parts of consciousness to leave the physical body and thus gain actual experience in the invisible worlds.[4] Many of the priests also knew how to use hypnotism, mesmerism, narcotic drugs, charms, talismans, fetishes, mantras, and could invoke elemental force. Any of these skills might have been used in various mysteries to test and to acquaint the pupil with the hazards and the possibilities in mortal and immortal existence.

It is said that even today every initiate, at a certain stage, undergoes leaving his physical body and having experiences in the invisible worlds. He then returns to continue serving others in his earthly life. This encounter, of course, changes his fear of death because he realizes that consciousness is a continuing process in different forms. He no longer views death as the end of life and intelligence, but rather as the beginning of a different spiritual state that he has earned by preceding action. Recognizing that every state is generated by former acts gives him incentive to improve his conduct.

Hindu-Buddhist Concepts of Unfolding Consciousness and Form

In Hindu thought Brahman, the invisible Oneness, is made manifest gradually in the mineral, vegetable, and animal kingdoms, stage by stage, birth after birth, evolving different forms in each of the three worlds. Man is born into the world of waking consciousness, in a physical body through which he gains experience with material forms. At death, he passes into another world with a body suitable for continuing development. Still later he passes into a third world with an even more subtle body and there gains more experience. Then he starts again this round of three. It is like being bound on a great wheel of cycles, birth after birth, until he no longer is bound by desires and sentient existence. When man no longer identifies himself with his physical body, his mind, or his desires, he becomes free from rebirths in these three worlds and passes into a state of bliss. This is the state which the Buddhists call "Nirvana."

Each experience sets up a sequence, a cause and its effects, which the Hindu and the Buddhist call "karma." Experiences, life after life, are the exact effects of the causes set up previously and thus earned. As man develops in experience he gains in consciousness until he expands to the Nirvanic-consciousness and is beyond need of the three worlds and the "Wheel of Rebirths."

In each world he comes in contact with regions of the universe which bring out latent powers within himself. Experience in the material world, with its pleasures and pain, gives invaluable training to the man whose consciousness focuses on the physical body and environment. Experience in the emotional and mental worlds develops his more subtle bodies which clothe his less visible forms of consciousness as emotions, mind, and intuition. At last, when he has developed most powers and has purified all parts, man will know that the Self of the Universe and his own Self are one. According to the Hindu view, this slow evolution might be shortened with great effort by means of the practice of yoga or the science of union. The Hindus developed a number of schools of yoga to guide man in this purpose; all the approaches lead to the union of the lower self with the Higher Self.

Four different methods of yoga were developed to fit the needs of the active, the reflective, the emotional, and the experimental. Active persons were taught to cultivate right thought and action in order to bring order and beauty to others. Reflective persons were eager for knowledge and reverenced law; they were attracted to methods teaching them to purify the mind and give others the truth. Emotional persons offered self to deity in devotion, seeking oneness in love of God and men. Experimental persons sought oneness by developing the highest qualities of mind, emotions, and body.

A guru or teacher guided the pupil in these methods. The teaching was intended to unfold the pupil's powers of consciousness of the subtler worlds of being. By evolving his inner faculties he could know, by means of personal observation, rather than by accepting reports from others. He could live in the inner worlds, use their laws and their powers, and thus be of greater use to his fellowmen. A guru might inspire and stimulate the faculties that a pupil already possessed because the pupil's faculties would tend to vibrate at a frequency in unison with those of his guru. The pupil's lower mind would gradually be elevated to the higher intellect; his emotions would become intuitional; and his self-will would become more nearly one with divine nature.

A guru might have a group of pupils who were learning definite laws, experimenting first in simple ways, then with one power after another, learning to use the powers of the higher worlds. Only a few pupils qualified for the tests and initiation. Exceedingly few so dedicated and disciplined themselves that they could take one initiation after another, gaining mastery in various ways, until they were known as "adepts" or "masters."

A medical student deals with that part of the human equipment which is dense enough to be visible to the eye. A less dense part of the physical body, called by some the "etheric double," is visible to clairvoyants who describe is as a violet-grey mist interpenetrating the denser body. Modern electronic lenses connected to high frequency generators can record this invisible part of the physical body. This vitality flows through the body and keeps it alive; it acts as a bridge between one's physical body and one's thoughts, feelings, and higher forces.

The etheric double extends several inches beyond the physical body. On its surface lie centers, or points of connection, which the Hindu calls "chakras," and through which energy flows from one of man's vehicles or bodies to another. Clairvoyants have described these centers or vortices of force. In the undeveloped man they are usually two-inch circular depressions near the surface, but in the developed man they are blazing whirlpools of radiation. Each vortex is connected by a tube-like structure to a point in the spine. Seven vortices are continually rotating, and the force from higher worlds flows into them. In undeveloped man the motion is relatively sluggish, whereas in the highly evolved man the force flows and moves rapidly.

Each of the chakras or "turning wheels," as the Hindu name implies, has a different function and radiation. The two lower chakras are chiefly employed to receive into the body the two polarized forces at the physical level, the vitality from the sun and the so-called "serpent fire" from the earth, or "kundalini force." The intermediate group of three centers contribute the force through personality: the lower emotional or astral through the third center, the higher astral in the fourth center, and the lower mind in the fifth center. These vortices, although located just outside the dense physical body, nourish certain nerve centers in the physical body. The sixth and seventh chakras are connected with the pituitary gland and the pineal gland and come into action only when a certain degree of spiritual development has been attained.[5]

The root chakra at the base of the spine distributes the kundalini force through the human body for daily activities. This force exists on all planes. In the physical body it flows along the nerves and is called "nerve fluid." But if this chakra were quickened, a tremendous force would flow upward in three strands, one through the central tube of the spinal cord and one through a strand on either side of it. The force winds from side to side up the cord, stimulating each of the chakras as it flows upward. The second etheric chakra, the sacral center, supplies vital energy to the nervous system from the sun. The third chakra, associated with the solar plexus, affects feelings and emotions. The fourth chakra, over the heart, receives impressions from higher astral forces. The fifth center, at the throat, receives impressions from mental forces. The sixth center, sometimes related to the "third eye," is between the eyebrows. The seventh chakra, at the crown, known as the "lotus of a thousand petals" because of its radiations, is the last to develop. These etheric chakras keep the physical body alive, but they may also be stimulated into full activity. Each of the etheric centers, when fully aroused, brings to physical consciousness the quality in its corresponding emotional or astral center.

In the long ages of evolution, the emotional or astral body was inert and only vaguely conscious. The kundalini force at the astral level passed through the astral centers and activated them, gradually enabling the person to travel astrally, to have deeper powers of feeling, and to hear and see, in the astral sense. Although the astral centers are activated in all developed peoples, we do not yet have awareness and conscious control at all levels.

The Hindu guru practices great care in guiding his pupil. Those who wish to accelerate their evolutionary development are guided individually. They are tested in such qualities as morality, purity, control, persistence, compassion, and many other traits, for there is grave danger in increasing powers before a pupil has developed adequate discernment and stability. Hindu literature gives obscure hints to aid those who are qualified to understand them, so the wisdom has been handed on from age to age, from nation to nation.

As man develops, his astral centers are quickened, but he is not conscious of them. In order to increase latent powers, the etheric centers are developed and the astral centers respond, giving the individual definite powers. The only way to achieve awareness in physical consciousness is by awakening each of the etheric centers in turn. Different schools of yoga guide their pupils in various ways. Information is guarded because of the extreme danger to anyone who might misuse the power.

It takes long determined effort to vivify the primary chakra. Its fiery potency is so tremendous that it can easily shatter an unprepared nervous system. It can also intensify negative qualities as strongly as it can intensify good qualities. Many have wrecked their lives by foolish experimentation without guidance from a qualified teacher: it should be remembered that a qualified teacher would never accept money for his guidance. The wise teacher stresses selfless conduct, purity, and right action in serving others. Such conduct gradually brings about changes in the functioning of these centers.

The kundalini force of the primary center awakens other centers. The other vortices bring into physical consciousness many types of awareness. The awakening of the second etheric chakra, the sacral center, enables the pupil to remember astral journeys; the vivifying of the third center over the solar plexus gives sensitivity to astral influences; the awakening of the fourth or heart center gives instinctive sympathetic pleasure and pain; the arousing of the fifth, at the throat center, gives clair-audient powers; the development of the sixth between the eyebrows, brings clairvoyance and also magnifying and diminishing "sight"; and the vivifying of the seventh chakra enables man to leave his body in full consciousness and then return. With full development, consciousness is continuous through sleeping or waking, through living or so-called death.

The wisdom of the ancient Hindu and Buddhist sages has been given to those few who could qualify for the great responsibility, in order to better the development of mankind.

Egyptian Hermetic Concepts of Unfolding Consciousness and Form

The wise men of the ancient lands bordering the Mediterranean recognized that many divinities, which the ignorant worshiped, were personified attributes of the one Creative Force. Students in those days exchanged the knowledge they possessed. Scholars came from many lands; they were not considered heretics if they studied with teachers of more than one belief, because they recognized the principles worshiped, not the names. They sought wisdom, and how it was described or named did not confuse them.

The fable of Isis and Osiris has been fantastically interpreted by Plutarch and others. As an initiate, Plutarch would have had to hide the meanings from casual students; he would only have hinted at the hidden meanings. Many scholars tried to interpret the myths and fables but looked on them with disdain and superiority. They missed the deeper implied significances.

The fable about the life, death, and resurrection of Osiris can be studied as a mystery teaching about the possibility of expanding the pupil's awareness. When Truth (Osiris) was dead or exiled into the invisible world, Typhon ascended the throne; then institutions dominated by greed, ruthlessness, and ambition obscured righteousness. Isis gathered the scattered consecrated initiates and searched for the "body of her lord" (Truth). By magic (for all initiate-priests used invisible power), Isis resurrected the dead god, Truth, and through union with him brought forth Horus, the Hawk with the all-seeing eye.

Ambitious Typhon again captured, killed, and scattered the fourteen parts of Osiris, dispersing the wisdom all over the earth. Then Isis and the mystery schools searched for ages to restore the wisdom, piece by piece, all except one part, the phallus, the Lost Word. The phallus, which was said significantly to have been swallowed by a fish, was the threefold generative power. By magic, again Isis reproduced the missing piece so the divine power of Osiris was restored.[6]

In all ages, religions have confided the real meaning and the higher truths only to those who were advanced and dedicated to serving humanity. There is little doubt that the Osirian cycle was an Egyptian initiatory drama. Wise men of the world journeyed to Egypt, staying twenty or thirty years to learn from these profound mysteries. Certainly a man such as Pythagoras would not have spent twenty-two years of his life studying in Egypt unless he were receiving the highest form of human knowledge.

The description of the earth as the underworld where a death-like sleep prevailed symbolized that man might rise from this lethargic, ignorant state to a higher understanding. It indicated that truth might be destroyed for a time, as was Osiris, but that truth would rise again and be preserved.

It is quite possible that the Great Pyramid was not an observatory or lighthouse, nor, as usually considered, the tomb of the Pharaoh Cheops. For instance, some say that the sepulchral vault was never completed. There is not proof even that the building was erected by Egyptians, for it lacks their usual mortuary art. The seashells embedded at the base of the Pyramid suggest it may have been erected by much earlier peoples and may be perhaps 100,000 years old.

The word "pyramid" signifies light or fire, thus is a symbolic representation of the one Divine Flame in all that lives. Others liken the pyramid to the universe, with the capstone as man; or mind might be the capstone of man; or spirit the capstone of mind. If it had been meant to be a symbol of the microcosm and of the macrocosm, the secret teachings of Osiris and solar energy appropriately depicted the universal sepulchre in which man is entombed and later resurrected. Manly Hall suggests:

> As a rough and unfinished rock, man is taken from the quarry and by the secret culture of the Mysteries gradually transformed into a trued and perfect pyramidal capstone. The temple is complete only when the initiate himself becomes the living apex through which the divine power is focused into the diverging structure below.[7]

If, as seems possible, the Great Pyramid was a chamber for mystery school initiations, the wise entered as men and walked out of the mysteries with the wisdom of God in their hearts. Here they met, face to face, the holy one who never left the house of wisdom. Here they found the gateway to the Eternal. Here the dying god rose again.

The Great Pyramid was dedicated to the God Hermes or Thoth, who personified Universal Wisdom. Entrance into the mysteries was not limited by race or creed. The only two qualifications were that the inquirer must live a clean life and that he must want the wisdom more than he wanted life itself. The wise ones came from afar to learn the hidden wisdom and to pass through the tests and rituals of initiation.

The labyrinth and subterranean passageways represented the journey through the sorrows, temptations, suffering, and confusions of earthly existence. Hades, Amenta and the Underworld were all names for that journey from cradle to grave, as traveled by those who wandered through life dominated by the senses. These were indeed in a sepulchre or cold coffin of self-limitation.

The Egyptian mysteries taught that there were two kinds of existence, one for those who are asleep and another for those who are awake. In a universe planned to provide opportunity for infinite growth, some exist in ignorance, in selfishness, and in egotism, unaware of change, development, and service. They are, indeed, sleeping or "dead," even though they walk on the earth. Their self-generated lower natures have brought them this limitation.

Those who are awake search for the light and make use of every opportunity. They progress toward wisdom, beauty, and the good. Gradually they unfold talent after talent and become master in one situation after another. The world and its problems are the laboratory in which men gain various strengths. They come to know themselves and to be conscious of the Self which is not the physical body, nor the emotions, nor the mind. They realize that body and form may change but that the Self is immortal. The consciousness of the Self eliminates death as the end and replaces it with the concept of changing forms.

In the mystery schools, a pupil might gain power and illumination, coming nearer the perfection of "the gods." As he realized the relation between the individual self and the Universal Self, he became more sensitive in using the divinity buried within himself.

The development of man's spiritual nature was not regarded as a haphazard process. Definite laws and procedures were taught. The secret process of resurrecting the divine nature in man was taught only to the worthy. A person entered the temple of initiation dedicated to service and consecrated to finding truth and wisdom. The depth and degree of this consecration determined whether his consciousness was ready to use greater wisdom. Great care was necessary in testing candidates because greater sensitivity might be dangerous, both to himself and to others, if prematurely given. The process of raising the consciousness or the "frequency" was guarded with the greatest secrecy in order to avoid misuse and great harm.

Those who came to the temple were put on probation while they prepared themselves. The ceremonies and rituals used by the Egyptians and other schools are not fully known, nor is the sacred process ever written down. *The Book of Thoth* is still in existence and contains some of the processes used for the regeneration of man. It is thought to describe the method of stimulating certain areas of the brain which extend consciousness.

Carefully guarded glyphs gave hints; when the time was judged right, the candidate achieved the ability for his consciousness to slip out of his physical body for experience on higher levels. Afterwards he returned to continue his earthly life, "resurrected" or "born again," but knowing actual immortality. He then knew death to be only change from a physical body to a finer frequency of consciousness. As a man learned to use this knowledge, and much more that was given him, his life became a great center through which power radiated to help mankind.[8]

Persian Zoroastrian and Mithraic Concepts of Unfolding Consciousness and Form

The Mithraic cult was a simplified form of the more ancient Zoroastrian fire magic. It taught its disciples and held initiations usually in underground caves which were decorated with signs of the Zodiac. The summer solstice of Cancer was regarded as the gate of the soul's entrance into earthly life, and the winter solstice of Capricorn as the gate through which the soul returned to the gods.

There were three degrees: one of self-purification, one of intellectual development, and one of control of the animal nature. At the first initiation the candidate was given a crown, the symbol that he was ruler of his own soul and must choose between the spiritual and the animal nature. In the second degree he wore the armor of intelligence and purity; he was tested in subterranean pits as he fought beasts of lust and passion. In the third degree he was robed with a cape on which were woven the signs of the zodiac and other astronomical symbols, signifying the mysteries giving the soul, in its highest form, a heavenly nature. Later he was greeted as one who had risen from the dead and was given secret instructions. After this initiation he was called a "Lion." Manly Hall gives reference

> . . . to the birth of Mithras as the Sun God, his sacrifice for man, his death that men might have eternal life, and lastly, his resurrection and saving of all humanity by his intercession before the throne of Ormuzd.[9]

The Mithraic cult did not reach as high philosophically as has the Zarathushtrian religion, yet its mystery teachings spread over the Roman Empire as far west as Germany, France, and Britain. Its influence has been reflected widely in Europe where many continue to aspire to the purity of fire, to recognize individual responsibility for development, and to change habits in refining their bodies.

Greek Orphic Concepts of Unfolding Consciousness and Form

Orpheus, whose origin is lost in time, was said to be the founder of Greek mythology. He used myths to express symbolically his great philosophic concepts. He derived some of his material from the Egyptians and, no doubt, some from the Brahmins. He was one of the many immortals who limited himself by descending to earth and sacrificing that mankind might have the wisdom of the gods.

The Orphic mysteries were concealed in the myth about Orpheus seeking Eurydice, who was imprisoned in the underworld. The legend represented, of course, a soul seeking experience and understanding in the limited physical universe. The Orphic reforms changed man's primitive notions about death; they abolished fears of the world of the "shades." Instead, man learned of a divine, benevolent plan for his destiny. Life had a logical purpose. Only the physical form died, not the soul. Life returned periodically to the material world for experience. The soul's desires, passions, and appetites depended upon physical life for their gratification; so until the soul overcame the desire for sensory experience, it would be pulled back to reincarnate. Until worldliness was no longer dominant, the cycle would continue, giving opportunity for development and experience. The Orphic mystery schools were established to purify man's nature that he might, during growth in many lives, eventually approach perfection.

Orpheus sang praises to the good and the beautiful. He presented the universe as one vast symphony of virtues, and taught that the Gods were to be worshiped with hymns of beauty and Harmony, meaning the Gods were venerated in the harmonic values which pattern daily life. The Orphic mysteries taught that man could liberate the forces within his own psyche by controlling and directing his dynamic energies. He might be thought of as a god functioning in the body of an animal until he developed his transcendent nature.

The Greeks believed that man had within himself a spark of vitality from the eternal. Orphic theology spoke of the organism and its functioning being "suspended" from the indestructible fire, and all modes of activity were expressions of the divine principle of spiritual intelligence. Rarefied matter between the material body and the immortal spirit linked the two extremes together into one unit. Ancient theology needed no outside "savior" or institution because the unity was always present within.

The "daimon" of Socrates has been translated in present psychological terms as part of the unconscious; "the gods," in general, as group consciousness. The ancient seers realized that the masses needed a concrete ideal for worship. The pantheon of "lesser gods" in various nature activities made the presence of God available in the heart of man's own nature. The Greeks recognized God in all manifestation, even in the lowest forms and acts of organic life.

They wisely reverenced the One God beyond the reach of thought. Their various forms of elemental forces were emanations from the One Cause. They did not deem it blasphemy to recognize themselves, nor the simplest forms active in nature, as part of the organism of their God. Discreetly, they left Absolute Deity beyond mental description but named the attributes of God in the variously described forms immediately within their own self or within their own environment. This immanent God was "closer than breathing, nearer than hands and feet." The germinal deity within, the potential, was there in the consciousness, buried within the sensual nature and the incessant flight of the mind. The Supreme God, the wholeness, was not within man, but only that ray of potential which each was capable of receiving. Lodged within each form of consciousness was the seed, the potential nucleus. In man, that divine nucleus was the Christos, the Son of the Almighty Father.

The ancient seers were deep students of man's constitution. They found human nature to be a compound of at least four segments, which functioned in different types of substance. The interaction of the several "men" which they found in a human being was the field of study from which they built an extensive catalogue of reactions in consciousness.[10] These ancient "psychologists" had names and descriptions of clearly defined states of subjective activity, some unknown to modern psychology. Their "gods" were living energies of mind and nature. Their terminology by no means invalidated their detailed classification or descriptions. The reactions which we term mystical were charted in relation to the whole being and were not based merely upon feelings. The re-examination of their findings shows that man need not be a victim of evolution, drifting unconsciously with the "tide of humanity," but that he may know the laws and work intelligently with a plan for a smooth, swift evolutionary advancement.

Usually man's consciousness is focused upon sense perceptions, so he is aware only of the physical body and nature. To become consciously aware in the other bodies is not a matter of distance but of vibrational frequencies. The Greek emphasis on harmonizing or matching the correspondences at different levels was an excellent way, at that time, to stress the harmonic intervals of bodies that have different frequencies.

The Greeks represented the different planes by five geometric figures: the cube for earth, the sphere for water, the triangle for fire, the crescent for air, and the candle-flame tip for aether (the next plane that was to be formed). But in much of their folklore these five symbols were simplified into the imagery of two: fire for the higher or divine segment, and water for the earthly man. With this simple key to their myths, many of their implied meanings become clear and significant.

The Eleusinian mysteries, founded about 1400 B.C., have been preserved to modern times mainly through the Platonic system. The initiates were known for their high moral practices and for the beauty of their philosophical concepts. Their rites interpreted nature mystically, giving precious secrets about Ceres and Bacchus. These secret concepts are believed to be branches of the earlier Isis and Osiris mysteries of Egypt. Their intellectual understanding of the One Source, of Light, and of Truth spread an influence through the known world.

The greater Eleusinian mysteries required a deep knowledge of Greek mythology for understanding the esoteric keys. The lesser mysteries, dedicated to Persephone, signified occultly the soul in an earthly body overcome by the animal nature and therefore wandering in darkness. The Eleusinian teaching was that man, the psyche, symbolized by Persephone, must rise above ignorance during his life. He must outgrow the desire for material possessions and all lesser values. If the psyche accepted the limitations and illusions of his human environment he would wander endlessly in lives and deaths until he attained spiritual awareness and was freed. Birth into ignorance in the physical world was considered a limitation and death. Plato described the body as a tomb. Philosophers taught that "the only true birth was that of the spiritual soul of man rising out of the womb of his fleshly nature."[11] They claimed that the majority of people were ruled, not by their higher living spirit, but by their animal personalities which the philosophers symbolized as living in the underworld of death. The Eleusinian mysteries survived all other mystery institutions and lasted until about 400 A.D.

Much of the greatness of Greece has been attributed to its religio-philosophic institutions. The temples of the mysteries represented the finest architecture and art in Greece. Besides being used for initiation rites, they were storehouses of literature from earlier times. Some of these temples had a seating capacity for as many as 25,000. They were the cultural centers of society.

The temples contained sound chambers, constructed for special purposes, to amplify intonements of invocations used in the mysteries. When the frequencies were repeated their influence was increased. Every element in nature and in every person was known to have a keynote, a combination of tones in a harmonic ratio. Resonance, the modern term, was studied and used by these early scholars.

The Greeks regarded the lyre as a sacred symbol of the human being. The body of the instrument was the physical form, the strings were the nerves, and the musician was the spirit. Thus playing upon the nerves, the spirit created harmonies. Plato estimated some exalted Egyptian songs and poems to have been in use at least 10,000 years; he thought the gods must have composed their harmonies.

As an initiate of the mysteries, Plato was sworn to secrecy concerning methods to regenerate man. Throughout his writings, however, are hints. First, man must actualize the reality of truth and dedicate his whole being and effort to integrity and virtue. The gods were the most perfect manifestation of truth. Next to the gods were listed heroes and enlightened men who had lifted themselves above the common man; they were less than the gods and more than mortals, so they were designated as demi-gods. All the rest of mankind and life forms, in which spiritual and divine principles were only slightly developed but were in no way dominant, Plato regarded as being in a body which he called "the sepulchre of the soul."

> All creatures in whom the higher nature is in servitude to the bodily impulses are properly termed dead, inasmuch as truth is dead within them, having no way of manifesting itself.[12]

Plato envisioned vast cycles of time as necessary for his concept of growth, change, and progression. All growth was a process of ascending. He did not mean the form, but the life progressing within the form. He taught reincarnation as a reasonable explanation of the mystery of life. The process of becoming extended over tremendous spans of time.

Socrates also realized that life was a continuum. He knew that by drinking the hemlock he would only change the form of his consciousness. Immortality did not depend upon preserving the physical body. Once having learned that one cannot die, and having gained consciousness of the Self, he could never lose consciousness even though his form would change. This realization of spiritual continuance enabled Socrates to drink the poison without hesitation.

Plato believed that the wise should be responsible for leading, instructing, and protecting the uninformed. He thought of the community as an organization established for service and cooperation. He believed the community could, by early training, teach children and citizens that the individual labors for the good of the whole group. It was an illusion for men to think of themselves as separate from each other. The life and purpose of each person was part of the whole society. The realization of this interdependent community existence, he believed, would develop man's mental equipment and put an end to social evils.

Plato said that learning was remembering, or reasoning from the unconscious wisdom learned in previous lives. He thought that the study of the arts refined the passions, that science developed reason, and that increased knowledge gave perspective and appreciation. He taught his pupils to accept nothing contrary to reason. He encouraged them to answer their own questions. With philosophically detached insight, they were to reason from the general to the particular, thus fitting small matters into order. If they perceived the one divine Principle which sustained all, they would understand the diversity of temporal forms and the truth manifesting as intelligence everywhere in nature. (Piaget and other educators have now proven that even children from five to seven years old have potential conceptual powers when challenged to use them.)

The Greek educational system included initiation into the state mysteries. The lesser mysteries were given quarterly, and anyone of good character might apply for initiation. Women and children above six years were admitted. The rituals were in the form of dramatic pageants. Those who excelled in the lesser mysteries might be chosen by the priests to compete for the greater mysteries. Tests for these included great physical, emotional, and mental dangers, so only those sound in body, stable in emotions, and wise in arts, sciences, and universal learning could succeed. Probably only a few hundred ever passed successfully into the greater mysteries.

Those who were initiated received secrets for personal development and the keys with which to interpret religious fables. Their internal development gave great dignity and power. They were the heroes, the demi-gods. They were honored in every home, and even princes and kings venerated them. Their vows of secrecy have been so preserved that the inner mysteries of their initiatory rites have never been exposed. Occasional hints may be found in literature, but their best registration has been in the lives of initiates such as Pythagoras, Plato, and Aristotle.

Christian and Post-Christian Concepts of Unfolding Consciousness and Form

The teachings of Jesus were similar to those of the preceding religions. Only the pure could see purity: "Blessed are the pure in heart; for they shall see God."[13] The teachings of the Manu, Zoroaster, Buddha, and Jesus each spoke of loving one's enemies and doing good to others.[14] Jesus also emphasized the oneness of light.[15] The straight and narrow gate[16] was described by others as the sharp razor-edged path. The great compassionate call "Come unto me"[17] to those who were heavily laden was a reiteration of the teachings of the Great Brotherhood of Adepts. The ancient teaching concerning the futility of attachments to things was told in the parable "Go and sell that thou hast."[18] The ancient law of cause and effect was recognized at the time of Jesus, who taught that man reaps as he sows.[19]

Many people believe now, as the ancient ones did, that consciousness is a continuum. In waking consciousness the perceptions come through the sensory apparatus of the physical body. In sleep the state of consciousness is said to divide into two parts, one repairing the physical body and the higher subtler part traveling in the astral, mental, or spiritual worlds. Upon the individual's waking, these parts are reunited. Some clairvoyants can "see" the physical body and its etheric parts as these separate and reunite. Through purity of living, service to humanity, meditation, and development, some, like the initiates of the mystery schools, have passed in waking consciousness into the astral, or mental, or spiritual worlds and have returned. They have learned that consciousness continues after death in a form that is much more free and more subtle than in the physical form.

Some of the early Christian writers said that after Jesus' resurrection he remained on earth for eleven years teaching the secret wisdom to his Apostles. According to Acts 1:3, Jesus remained only forty days instructing the disciples about the unwritten wisdom of the kingdom of God. This implies that the Master Jesus functioned in a body more subtle than the physical. The masses were not yet prepared for an advanced teaching. Therefore, as Origen states, Jesus conversed with his disciples in private, teaching the knowledge that was not written. Even St. Paul, writing to the Church at Corinth, stated:

> I, brethren, could not speak to you as unto spiritual, but as unto carnal, even as unto babes in Christ.[20] . . . We speak the wisdom of God in a mystery, even the hidden wisdom . . . we speak wisdom amongst them that are perfect [more developed].[21]

Clement of Alexander stated that the benefits of the wisdom should not be communicated to those who were unpurified in soul nor should the teachings be given to the profane.[22] [23] Origen explained that the Christian doctrine was not secret but that beyond the exoteric teachings were others which could be understood only by those who had higher stages of development.

The long, severe training necessary to achieve the ability to leave the physical body consciously and to experience higher, fuller consciousness was not popular. The life of Christ, as given in the Bible, presents the universal path of initiation, not a historical, personal biography. The mystery drama was used to teach the people about transcending the personal (being crucified, dying) and attaining higher consciousness (being resurrected), but the pupil did not experience the reality of the superphysical. The student received only intellectual and emotional training without the disciplines to unfold higher senses and bodies. Formerly the true initiate had gained firsthand knowledge as he himself traveled through superphysical worlds and experienced survival in different states of consciousness and form. These later generations gained knowledge only vicariously as their drama and their literature used animals to symbolize overcoming of animal passions and attaining virtue.

When science was gaining strength by using direct experience, the church was excluding as heretics those who had attained mystical knowledge through direct experience. The Church Fathers declared that all spiritual knowledge was within the reach of those who had faith, even though they were ignorant. This doctrine alienated those with great knowledge who recognized that both information and purity are necessary for spiritual development.

The early church struggled between superstition and knowledge. The masses of Christians had very little knowledge. The more educated, known as Gnostics, tried to introduce some of their convictions into the church, for they saw exclusive narrowing tendencies growing in the young organization. Passionate devotion to the personal Christ developed the heart but not the mind. Faith was not superior to knowledge; both were needed. Outstanding writings of this early period of Christianity, such as the *Pistis Sophia* and the translation of the *Divine Pymander,* retained the occult mystery teachings but unfortunately were not studied by most Christians.

The Greek armies of Alexander the Great brought back some of the Hindu philosophy to the Hellenic states. The Romans, too, contributed a broad perspective, for the soldiers were influenced by those they conquered. Rome maintained a democratic attitude toward all conquered territories and became the city of many cultures and philosophies. Plato's mature doctrine of religious unity, along with his reasoning from a general concept to particulars, had great influence upon a group of thinkers who followed this period.

The Neo-Platonists realized that a basic unity underlay all religions. They accepted the concept that unity was the reality and diversity an illusion. All the diversity of form in religions had come from one foundation. They taught that the supreme power of good was an expression of superior being or principle and that prophets, saviors, and saints revealed this power to man. They taught that man was an immortal spirit in a physical form and that at death he continued as a spiritual creature with various opportunities according to merits earned in his earth life. Messiahs appeared on earth to aid the people in their growth and to venerate the Supreme Being.

During the Dark Ages in Europe the influence of the Neo-Platonic School of thinking passed from Christian countries to Arabic peoples and to Islamic custody. The Neo-Platonic philosophers taught that the gods were modes of universal thought or degrees of awareness. Life was divided into degrees of self-awareness and universal awareness. Man's growth was measured by his awareness of the universal from which he was suspended.

In education the Neo-Platonists emphasized that it was not what was taught but how it was taught that was significant. A speaker's intent was more essential than what he said. A pupil could acquire abstract truths only by inner experience in consciousness. The Neo-Platonists elevated the mind to merge with causes rather than with differences in detail. In politics they dreamed of a world democracy in which each nation contributed as it could. Man's primary objective was to attain a state of enlightenment. Possessions, as everything else, should be held in moderation. Beauty was order and harmony suspended from the universal pattern.

When religion gave up its primary purpose of illuminating man and replaced it with political domination, it forfeited the confidence of thinking people. As a result, a great conspiracy was hidden by elaborate symbolic devices in manuscripts and in secret codes. There were a great number of societies of pre-Reformation reformers. Because they were persecuted, they scattered over the entire European continent. One writer recounts that in the middle of the thirteenth century about four thousand higher initiates of these esoteric groups were wandering about Europe, disguised as troubadours, peddlers, merchants, and journeymen.

About this time craftsmen and artisans perfected the printing trade. The new crafts of printing and papermaking led to the publication of innumerable books and pamphlets, some of which dealt with magic, alchemy, cabalism, Rosicrucianism, and various reforms in art and science. Authors were unknown, curious symbols were used, and ciphers covered meanings. The printers and bookbinders belonged to a secret order dedicated to spreading truth in order to uplift man. Neither bribery nor coercion could force the printer to reveal the source of his materials. The cost of publishing such books would have been prohibitive unless it had been a labor performed for love of humanity.

Many of the lighter works which appealed to the people were fables filled with social and political significance and tinged with heresy. "Reynard the Fox" for instance, was most popular in Europe. Such a childish story was enjoyed because adults substituted heresy for the fox and Rome for the wolf. No doubt the troubadours or some such order created these tales to give discomfort to an order of monks. Satires and illustrations attacking the privileged classes emphasized equality, democracy, and freedom.[24]

The guilds acted as a link between the trade unions and the troubadours. The secrets of the various crafts were guarded along with concealed mysticism. The universal mystery was hidden in the art and language of each guild. Almost all of the guilds were more than trade unions since they hid some trace of "heresy."

The troubadours acted as tutors of chivalry and therefore taught the youth. This was one of the best opportunities to change world opinion. Outwardly they taught the genteel way of life, but also they taught the rights of man and service for the common good as man's highest calling. They sang children's fairy tales but adapted them to their own purposes. Their philosophical fraternity was consecrated to the discovery of the powers of heart and mind necessary to bring universal reform to mankind.

The troubadours' passionate ballads, addressed to the fair ladies of their hearts, disguised their gospel of the divine love of God for man and the human love which could bring brotherhood. Only initiates realized that the "fair lady" was Isis, the world wisdom, and that their "Court of Love" was world democracy.[25] The Church and State were aware of threatening rebellion and set up the Inquisition to preserve their social structure and to destroy those who plotted against temporal and ecclesiastical autocracy.

The minnesingers, members of the gentry, and the meistersingers, middle-class hard-working craftsmen, formed cooperatives to protect members from all kinds of exploitation. These small self-governing groups also concealed the dream of universal brotherhood. The Knights Templars retained more of the Eastern mysteries but were suppressed by the Inquisition, perhaps in part to confiscate the great wealth of the Templars.

After the Knights Templars were destroyed, the esoteric students cautiously used the unique terminology of astrologers, alchemists, cabalists, Rosicrucians, and Masons. Thus the secret wisdom was preserved and the work of initiates was described in various ways in literature as that of world heroes and defenders of the weak. The knight was dedicated to serving afflicted and exploited human beings. He was dedicated to rescuing his own soul, "the fair maiden in distress," by overcoming the dragons, giants, and wicked nobles who robbed the poor. The legends of chivalry were covered accounts of the search for truth and the rituals of secret societies which promoted human emancipation.

"The Mother of the Mysteries," "Virgin of the World," was a concept veiled under Shakespeare's lady in his sonnets and Dante's Beatrice. The "Courts of Love" were believed to have inspired St. Francis of Assisi and Richard the Lion-hearted. The lady whose name must not be spoken was served by the gallant knights of whom the minnesingers sang.

The contributions of Charlemagne and his twelve peers, the legends of Roland, King Arthur and his Round Table, Wagner's Parsifal, Hercules, Siegfried, Robin Hood—the list of world heroes is long, but examined closely similar patterns are disclosed. The story of the various heroes evidences a continuing secret organization and plan for enlightenment and reform.[26] Like the Brotherhood of the Himalayas or the Egyptian Trismegistus, whose art was the perfecting of man through internal illumination, so too, the writers worked to perfect nature through divine art. The alchemists and astrologers formed a bridge between ancient magic and modern science. At that time, most of the chemists were also alchemists, most of the astronomers also practiced astrology, and most mathematicians and physicists speculated in metaphysical abstractions.

The mystical-chemical societies disintegrated only to form new organizations. The transmutation of metals in the old symbolic terminology was not lost, for the transmutation of man himself continued. The adepts turned to current needs, which are social. The opening of the Western Hemisphere gave utopian hope that the new world of brotherhood was at hand.

The outer circumstances of events in the lives of great men seem so different that it is no wonder historians and writers of biography failed to discern the possibility of a great inner trend of events unfolding a carefully laid plan. But if one studies the motive behind works of such men as Roger Bacon, Paracelsus, Jacob Böhme, St. Germain, Cagliostro, Francis Bacon, Sir Isaac Newton, Benjamin Franklin, and many others, it seems possible that they were influenced by similar ideals and that they may well have been members of secret societies promoting individual illumination for world betterment.

The purpose of most medieval thinkers and Renaissance intellectuals was directed toward man's personal interests. The church taught that Divine Will decreed all that happened, so the people had no incentive for social welfare. But the voyage of Columbus brought new hope to the people, and the Protestant Reformation broke the centuries of self-imposed delusion over the authority of the clergy which had limited man. An age of exploration followed, freeing the intellect to discover the mysteries and the world. This trend was aided by various writers of extravagant utopian fiction, much of which was similar to Plato's *Empire of the Philosophic-Elect.*

The Royal Society of London was acknowledged to have been patterned upon Lord Bacon's concepts. Careful study indicates that many of the perplexing unknowns of the Middle Ages and Renaissance periods could be aligned logically into a continuing motive secretly to aid man's development.

In modern times esoteric study and growth appeals to those who have attained a certain type of development. The masses in the universities and churches still disparage the emphasis of liberal universal thinkers. Nevertheless, changes both in form and in consciousness are coming more rapidly as the twentieth century closes. Man's physical, emotional, and intellectual development render outmoded the sectarianism and proselytizing of the past. The contribution of each religious emphasis is coming to mean part of world thought. There is a trend for people to be accepted, not for their faith or race, but for their intrinsic worth. Nations are trying to unite for world betterment—the dream of great men through the ages. More individuals are accepting responsibility for their actions. More are challenged to speed up the long evolutionary climb by persistent disciplines of selfless service and by meditation. More are avoiding glamour and the search for flashy superficial phenomena. And private intuitional instruction of the more mature members of society is still given when the pupil's equipment is ready for a higher state of consciousness.

The Great Ones need dedicated workers to aid humanity. Growth must be at all levels, and only advanced disciples safely use psychic sensitivities, after they have gained control of lower powers. Sensory and extrasensory perceptions, such as clairvoyance, classify and divide; but spiritual vision brings a unified understanding. The advanced disciple tries to keep the channel of communication open between the inner awareness and the brain so that impressions from the Great Universal may come through the mind. By quieting his mind through meditation and right action, he increases receptivity and attunement to higher levels.

Often it is the pupil's own soul, "the Master in his own heart," which communicates to him. He may flatter himself by thinking he is influenced by the group with whom he associates or that his "Master" speaks to him, but such an interpretation might only indicate ambition and a selfish desire for attention.

Mature disciples, dedicated to service, fulfill their obligations, and carry forward their "Master's work" in order to conserve his energies. They do not expect interviews and phenomenal contacts. The work done is for humanity and in no way for personal satisfaction. The pupil is not even assured of his own progress in the work except for inward signs which are almost imperceptible. Those who would be instruments of transmission for the higher forces must live pure regulated lives and must have disciplined bodies and minds, a sense of proportion, wholehearted devotion to mankind, and appreciation for the highest values.

In various ways a Great One knows the worthiness and needs of the volunteer for service. He has ability to "see" a glow or radiance from the head of an aspirant. He also may examine the karmic record which the aspirant must fulfill. This record will show service rendered the world.[27] Prerequisites to usefulness are a healthy body, emotional stability, fine mental equipment, and alignment of the ego and its Higher Self.

The three etheric force centers below the diaphragm are most active in average man. As they are reorganized from positive activity to negative functioning, the four etheric force centers above the diaphragm change from a negative state to a positive functioning. Man's reorganization of the lower centers, transferring the positive energy into the higher centers, is accomplished by character building and purification of bodies used in the three worlds. His awakening of the upper centers and bringing them to a positive state of functioning is accomplished naturally through meditation and organized daily purpose.

Forced drastic changes, as encouraged by some fanatical idealists, can be exceedingly dangerous. Overemphasis and lack of balance can cause great harm. Change must come slowly and sanely, guided by logical reason, intuition, and spiritual perception. The latent energies at the base of the spine will be lifted to the head; the energies of the sacral center, formerly used in physical creation, will be reoriented to the throat center; and the energies focused formerly at the solar plexus, expressing emotion and the desire nature, will be reoriented to the heart center.[28] When these balances are gradually accomplished, the changes in the head center and in new states of consciousness will make the pupil far better equipped to aid mankind.

Many are lured to seek psychic powers for self-assertion rather than to give special service to humanity. Those who will exploit such selfish interests and sidetrack the pupil from safe, true development are numerous. Usually curiosity about psychic phenomena is used to entice these pupils into detours of self-seeking, for a price.

Those who partially paralyze their physical equipment in trance, or by holding the breath in various breathing exercises, or by staring at a spot and failing to blink, or by other ways of forcing centers to awaken prematurely, do develop psychic abilities of a negative type. They are awakening primitive capacities of clairvoyance and function without control at emotional levels.[29]

Primitive consciousness was centered in the sympathetic nervous system and nerve plexuses (points of contact between the emotional and physical bodies). The popular methods for developing clairvoyance give quick, easy reversion to primitive clairvoyance at an emotional level without control.

Each person is a medium in the sense that each may be affected by and may transmit the thoughts of others. Mediumship is passive, but positive clairvoyance is an actively controlled agent. As man developed the cerebrospinal nervous system, the mental capacity dominated over the emotional-feeling capacities, and the sympathetic nervous system gradually became automatic and subconscious as the mind grew in complexity.

It is unfortunate that most people do not recognize the difference between primitive clairvoyance (based on emotion and uncontrolled) and positive clairvoyance (controlled by mental and spiritual development). Most people do not differentiate between a mind stilled by controlled conscious direction and a mind stilled by inhibition or partial paralysis or fatigue. There are many stages of psychic development. The sincere pupil must learn to discern between quick, easy reversion to primitive capacities and those methods which give control for uses in the betterment of mankind.

During the last century vast records of psychic research have accumulated. Unfortunately this work has usually been done with mediums, clairvoyants, telepathic sensitives, and others who had little or no control over these capacities. (Men obedient to absolute altruism and utterly committed to truth and loving service, those whose self-directed control enable them, are challenged in other forms of aiding mankind.) Furthermore, most psychical researchers have had little systemized or comprehensive theory of the phenomena they explore. There has been little willingness to investigate the knowledge ancient seers used. This closed-minded attitude has limited Western research into paranormal areas and has limited our knowledge of man's latent abilities.

REFERENCES

[1] Annie Besant, *The Changing World* (London: The Theosophical Press, 1909) pp. 161-166.

[2] Annie Besant, *A Study in Consciousness* (Los Angeles, California: The Theosophical Publishing House, 1918) p. 135 and pp. 128-129.

[3] Sri Madhava Ashish, *Man, Son of Man* (Wheaton, Ill.: The Theosophical Publishing House, 1970) p. 216.

[4] Manly P. Hall, *The Phoenix* (Los Angeles, California: The Philosophical Research Society, 1956) p. 35.

[5] C. W. Leadbeater, *The Chakras* (Madras, India: The Theosophical Publishing House, 1947) pp. 18-25.

[6] Manly P. Hall, *Freemasonry of the Ancient Egyptians* (Los Angeles, California: Philosophical Research Society, 1952) p. 73.

[7] Manly P. Hall, *The Secret Teachings of All Ages* (Los Angeles, California: Philosophical Research Society Press, 1945) p. XLIV.

[8] Hall, *op. cit., The Phoenix,* pp. 168-173.

[9] Hall, *op. cit., The Secret Teachings of All Ages,* p. XXIV.

[10] Alvin Boyd Kuhn, *The Lost Light* (New York, N.Y.: Columbia University 1940), pp. 264-265.

[11] Hall, *op. cit., The Secret Teachings of All Ages,* p. XXIX.

[12] Manly P. Hall, *Twelve World Teachers* (Los Angeles, California: The Philosophers Press, 1937) p. 157.

[13] Matt. 5:8.

[14] Matt. 44:45.

[15] Matt. 6:22-23.

[16] Matt. 7:14.

[17] Matt. 11:28-30.

[18] Matt. 19:16-24.

[19] Rev. 13:10.

[20] I Cor. 3:1.

[21] I Cor. 3:6-7.

[22] Stromata, 1:1.

[23] Stromata, 5:9.

[24] Manly P. Hall, *The Adepts—Order of the Quest* (Los Angeles, California: The Philosophical Research Society, 1945) pp. 23-30.

[25] *Ibid.,* p. 46.

[26] *Ibid.,* p. 41.

[27] Alice A. Bailey, *A Treatise on White Magic* (New York, N.Y.: Lucis Publishing Co., 1957) p. 183.

[28] *Ibid.,* p. 192.

[29] Irving S. Cooper, *Methods of Psychic Development* (Wheaton, Illinois: The Theosophical Press, 1946).

Chapter 7

TEACHERS GUIDE EVOLUTION

Levels of Consciousness

The superconscious state which transcends waking, dreaming, or sleeping states confers a purity of vision capable of perceiving Divine or Cosmic Intelligence. Man's latent higher consciousness, when it awakens, takes him beyond knowledge to a measure of infinite wisdom. The human personality now seems the most important part of man because his consciousness is focused in his physical body, in his sense organs, desires, emotions, and mind.

Those who consider that the cells of the physical body change every few years while the ego continues as an entity recognize that the physical body is only "an aspect of the total being"; that "mind and consciousness transcend physical limits."[1] Such people have but little difficulty envisioning man as being equipped with different kinds and degrees of organic coordination, or as having several types of bodies at different levels of development; to them it is reasonable that the arrangement of similar particles at different frequencies yields different bodies.[2]

Scientists are finding different force fields, each of which has laws that are unique to its areas. The study of the gravitational, electromagnetic, and nuclear force fields will probably be followed by proof of the existence of still other force fields in which universal laws function at their levels. Similarly, areas of consciousness which have unique behavior and laws, occultists classify as different levels of consciousness. To become aware at various levels of consciousness, and to master the laws focused in the emotional, mental, and spiritual bodies, seem part of the evolutionary process.

The Inner Teacher

Those who through persistent study obtain superior knowledge, and those who through persistent meditation become truly receptive, find within themselves an inner teacher, an awareness which guides them to increasing knowledge and wisdom. Only when the pupil has developed sufficient sensitivity to this intuitive communication is he equipped for still higher guidance. Gradually man develops conscious self-awareness at each level and recognizes his responsibility for self-direction. He then works in the more fully awakened spiritual state which the adepts and teachers of humanity have already achieved.

In Indian literature teachers are called "gurus," "rishis," "arhats," whereas in the West they are usually called "adepts." Such teachers usually live in some secluded place instructing their disciples. They are masters of religious philosophy and the esoteric sciences. Their basic purpose is to teach mankind and, if a pupil proves worthy, to lead him to cleanse the body and mind of limitations so he may gain intuition or be united with his own divine nature. The seeker for truth is first a disciple of some learned teacher. As the student's ability increases he is guided to properly cultivate his spiritual faculties. When he has developed the requisite abilities he may participate in a symbolic initiation or ritualistic drama. In this he is said to personify the process unfolding within him and about him. The pupil is then ready for even more development in consciousness.

Gautama Buddha, A Great Teacher

Gautama Buddha first gave his teachings to the five ascetics who had been his former companions. As he delivered his first sermon they listened from a distance but soon came near. They became the first monks of the Sangha order. Buddha then traveled along the

Ganges valley giving discourses to the growing numbers of disciples who followed him. After six years he returned to the city of his birth. By this time, hundreds of disciples followed him. During his discourses Buddha often referred to events that had happened in his previous incarnations. These accounts were carefully collected by his disciples. They tell of unselfish service for mankind's improvement. His sermons and discourses were memorized by his disciples and many of the Sutras were revealed during his long pilgrimages as a teacher. He had no desire to start a new religion but wished only to free the people from superstition and formalism in the current Hindu practices.

The Buddhist scriptures were written down several hundred years after his death, and gradually Buddha was deified as were other Buddhas and their Bodhisattvas. The doctrine spread to the South and the North and to many other countries. According to the 1967 Encyclopaedia Britannica *Book of the Year,* there are now approximately 13,382,000 believers. There are many branches of Buddhism and many interpretations given in the literature about Buddha and Buddhism.

Guatama Buddha came to reform Hinduism by teaching the Middle Way, so the teachings could spread into many lands. Previously, he is said to have incarnated as Vyasa, as Hermes, as the first Zoroaster, and as Orpheus; and then in India for forty-five years he taught again those whom he had trained in the previous ages.[3] When Gautama became the Lord Buddha his responsibility of teaching was given to the Bodhisattva, Lord Maitreya, whom we in the West call "the Christ." This great being is said to direct all educational and religious activities in the world through many personalities and agencies.

Jesus As Master Teacher and Guide

The Master Jesus knew that pupils must learn at their own level. He taught the multitudes separately from the more advanced students, using parables about nature and familiar objects. Most of the masses were uneducated and needed simple social and ethical concepts. To surmount this limitation and to instruct them at their level, yet to speak also to the better informed, he used an allegorical form of speech which narrated profound spiritual truths in an historical manner. He spoke to his disciples saying, "Unto you it is given to know the mystery of the kingdom of God, but unto them that are without all these things are done in parables."[4]

This special type of language, although based upon historical event, had double and triple and sometimes sevenfold meanings. The more advanced mysteries were comprehended only by those who were ready. Jesus knew the value of right timing and appropriate levels of instruction. He said, "Give not that which is holy unto the dogs, neither cast ye your pearls before swine, lest they trample them under their feet."[5]

Jesus recorded historical events with a symbolic sacred language which revealed deep underlying truths concerning laws of creation, of life, of healing, and of fulfillment. Significant meanings may be understood if one studies the parable or teaching thoughtfully and intuitively. For instance, some of the recorded events may be considered as universally continuing experiences occurring subjectively in man. They may describe inner experiences by using an outer event. Eternal values may be found, such as supersensory states and inner mystical experiences. Sometimes also concepts are personified in parables to signify man's nature. Many a story is a graphic description of man's evolutionary development. Also, many objects used in the Bible have symbolic meanings that are common to sacred writings of other religions and that imply similar hidden concepts. Much care was taken to protect against misusing wisdom which could give great power for good or likewise great destructive power.[6]

Bible events which seem ridiculous or impossible have been found to highlight most significant deeper truths; thus the pupil who has only superficial understanding is baffled, and only the student with highly intuitive insight discerns the deeper hidden essence.

Jesus understood that his pupils needed time to digest the wisdom as shown by, "I have yet many things to say unto you, but ye cannot bear them now."[7] He taught the esoteric wisdom to the few who were advanced even as had the Hebrews with their Cabala and other ancient mystery schools. The exoteric knowledge was given to the many, but the esoteric was never put in written form. It was given by direct instruction and by symbols which required a knowledge of the keys or was meaningless.

The Master Jesus taught, as had great ones who preceded him, that "I and My Father are one."[8] St. Paul said, it is the "Christ in you, the hope of glory."[9] And again, "One God and Father of all, who is above all, and through all, and in you all."[10] This inseparable spiritual oneness is yet to be realized, but a great many forces are now emphasizing convergence in Christian and other world religions.

Other Teachers Throughout The Ages

Some religions have taught people to seek God for His help, but great beings are always radiating help to mankind. It is man's own personality which limits their inflowing force; it is personality which separates self from Deity. Until the personality recognizes that its own soul infuses and creates all forms of impelling action, until the personality opens itself receptively, the potency and harmony of Deity is limited. We attain this soul identification on the inner levels of our being, for it exists as a subjective reality long before it manifests in our personality development as physical, emotional, and mental achievement.

There are many kinds of teachers during life. The

impact that modern science is making on mass understanding is as yet not widely comprehended. Relatively few are yet aware of the significance achieved when scientists recognized that the electron is an immaterial wave, not just a "particle," and that the atom is a force field in which ethereal electrons orbit around a nucleus at tremendous speeds.

It is difficult, as yet, for us to realize that all forms and objects in our universe are not solid but are basically invisible force. We have not yet had time to instill into our habit of thought the concept that invisible forces are the base of everything we see. The ancient ones had this training; for instance, the material world to the ancient Egyptians was the underworld, Amenta, because they believed all physical form emerged first from the invisible higher worlds. It remains for us to consciously train ourselves to an awareness that subtle energies underlie all forms of life. For most of us this is a difficult transitional period to surmount. It is a task which in the busy, active, heavy-laden lives that we live seems almost impossible.

The scientific concept that the universe is no longer in space but is identical with space makes the universe a wholeness, a One, quite beyond human comprehension, yet one in which all parts are interrelated. Such a oneness, in which all natural laws perpetuate that unity, and in which all consciousness and form are vital to that whole, indicates a God concept that is all-inclusive, even though it is not so labeled.

The recent scientific hypothesis of a universe oscillating endlessly in tremendous cycles of expansion and contraction is in accord with all other cyclic activities apparent in nature. Such a law of periodicity is not said to include an Absolute Reality or a superphysical One, as did the ancient Hindu idea of the "Nights and Days of Brahma," yet the hypothesis of the oscillating universe is in many respects so similar to the teaching of the ancient seers that it may eventually suggest further investigation of other common cyclic activities, such as birth and death, and the possible order and direction implied in all cyclic activity.

Newton advanced knowledge by inquiring about the invisible force which the moon, earth, and sun exerted upon each other. He observed that it was not mechanical but real, nonmaterial, and supersensible. J.C. Maxwell, in 1870, advanced knowledge by "thinking of space not as empty but as a fullness." Since about 1925, advances in science have changed belief to an exact knowledge of the nonmaterial reality which is the unmanifested source of all that exists in our world. Most people do not yet realize this tremendous change from belief to knowledge because for so long man has relied upon his sense perceptions as if they were the reality.[11] Nevertheless, our scientists are certain that nonmaterial, gravitational, and electromagnetic fields will sustain the astronauts in space.

In the everyday world we think in terms of individual units, such as events and objects, and these we later classify. Such emphasis on the separate individual is typical of everyday problem solving and of classical physics. Quite another way of studying relationships is that emphasized by modern "field theory" physics in which the most significant aspect of an entity is its part in a larger pattern. Each entity is observed only as a subsystem of a larger conceptual whole; each individual part exists and is part of that whole. Such large continuous fields may not be mechanically explicable, but observing them helps us answer some of our questions.[12]

Each of these ways of thinking may be useful in examining different types of problems, but they reach different conclusions and different ways of organizing reality. Causation, time, and space attributes change in essential structure when we regard them as segments in a continuum. The way of thinking which emphasizes time, history, and perception of individual characteristics gives man a comprehension of life, but just as valid is the way of thinking in terms of timelessness and eternity. These are two complementary views supplementing each other; the knowledge given by our senses is complemented by intuitive knowledge. Each way of thinking has its values and limitations. The patterns of particles which are finer than the atom are now being studied. The experimentation with such subatomic particles may lead to awareness of perception at even more subtle levels such as astral forms.

The viewpoint which relates only boundary lines, points, and surfaces limits one to geometric structural concepts. The viewpoint which goes beyond the geometric to boundless concepts implies that all entities are part of the total time-space continuum and are functioning at many different states in that continuum. This concept would modify our ordinary views of annihilation and creation because we would regard all entities, units, and objects as existing in the total field. Biological death is only a changed state in such a continuum; our limited perceptual range does not modify the invariance in the continuum. Entities or objects might change from one state into another, but the fact that we do not see them does not end their existence in reality. In field theory psychology it is essential not to confuse the structure with the function.[13]

Man Assumes A New Role

J. Krishnamurti, an internationally known thinker, emphasizes that people avoid responsibilities they should meet. No longer should man rely upon guidance from without as upon books and teachers, but each student should study his own beliefs, his direction, his way of believing, and learn why he clings to beliefs, for his "experience is shaped by belief."[14] That which man aspires toward he tends to become. Belief forms experience and his ideals; even "the belief in the Master creates the Master."

Our desires and our cravings cause conflict and suffering in our lives. We try to avoid the results of our desires by various self-deceptions; we strive to avoid misery by substituting reliance on books, lectures, a teacher, or a master, or by activity in political or charitable organizations, or by rituals, or by other forms of discipline. As we become identified with an idea, belief, group, or master, we attain a certain security, for there is a psychological reassurance even in being lost with the crowd. Our minds, focused on experience, cling to it for respectable power and pleasure. But such knowledge and experience is not reality. Both must cease if one would find the real.[15] In clinging to security, to the known, our mind forms a division between the real and ourselves; we make the separation within ourselves by the conflict of our opposing desires.

The mind makes many such divisions. Classifications, such as hierarchies of development, are in one sense illusions, because reality does not exist in degrees. There can be no spiritual distinctions; such degrees and distinctions are worldly titles and classifications. We are increasingly challenged with the need to know ourselves and to be aware of how our mind works if we would avoid illusion.

Man no longer depends upon Deity with awe and fear. His role has changed from passive acceptance to cooperative, creative action. He has learned, through modern science, to understand nature; through technology, to consciously guide natural processes and control his environment. He is no longer at the mercy of natural forces. He changes minerals and plants into endless varieties of goods, he builds cities and roads, he produces food in jungles and deserts, he controls disease, he transports ideas and products with increasing rapidity, he partially controls nature's rhythms with temperature and speed. His sense of dependence has changed.[16]

Man no longer uses ritual and belief systems to gain security. Instead, he is challenged to cooperate with natural laws, to be one with the ordered sequences, and to help create fulfillment. Religious practices and rituals are used quite differently from the past. Now a ritual is used as a harmonizing agent. Man's greater knowledge of that which is greater than himself gives him awe based upon his perception of infinite magnitude and ordered progression of a continuum. Man's fears stem from his own possible misuse of power rather than from Deity. The fears that plague him are unemployment and automation, or the prospect of becoming only a depersonalized number in a changing over-populated world, or of nuclear suicide, or of hunger, or of loss of freedom. All these he recognizes as man-made.

Man has assumed a new role. The sense of creating the future challenges him to understand details in the immediate sphere of cause and effect. The average man spends most of his life dealing with immediate technologies, obsessed with the practical applications of his concrete skills. Knowledge of ultimate realities, universal trends, purposes, and ordered abstractions have not usually been presented in a form that stimulates his abstract thinking. This void and imbalance lies back of much modern insecurity and strife.

Man needs to express vital action-values in daily living as his human capacities become more definitely organized. If he is to survive, man must ground his action in inclusive organic coordination; he cannot think and feel one way and act another way. The old idea of individuality is being outmoded and being replaced by a sense of larger relationships. We need to study the primary activities of the human brain-mind to find our unconscious tendencies, the role played by thought and feeling in shaping our lives. These most researchers have failed to study.[17] The insight of youth is bringing us face to face with this challenge.

Young people's vitality to explore capacities latent in man and their search for excitement both indicate a healthy state indispensable to growth. Unwilling to accept the status quo and separative values of the past, and unwilling to accept authority from others, youth gives promise of a future in which transformed social values will converge, making a social unity formed by appropriate variety. A man's deep desire to find a union in contrasts and an organic philosophy gives him the capacity to build tomorrow's values by his action.

Typically, people tend to go to extremes in tearing down an old established order before they find equilibrium in a new order. Driven by compulsion, by obedience to blind ignorance, by desperation, by lack of sympathy, and by a ruthlessness called "liberty," their uncontrolled extremes quickly become license expressing selfishness, greed, animal lusts, tyranny, and cruelty in bloodshed more violent than the order they are revolting against.

Nevertheless, this does not mean that values of the past are lost or that our civilization crumbles; rather it is the usual pattern found when the old order is replaced by a new one in a higher cycle. The confusion that occurs when one great evolutionary cycle is replaced by another may be long or short, depending upon man's reaction to change. If mankind could face his mistakes and rectify them honestly and courageously, if he could willingly pay the full price for his ignorance and selfishness, the new order would be established rapidly. The ancient glyph representing the closing of an old cycle and the forming of a new one shows a serpent swallowing or biting his own tail.

Man is capable of understanding nature and himself. He not only understands intellectually and analytically, but also intuitively. The balanced understanding which includes the intuitive, creative process requires a unified knowledge of the universe and man's place in it. Man must learn to think properly if he is to experience a unified knowledge and order. He must appreciate the continuity in all phases of the universe if he is to understand his relation to it.

Dr. Nikolai Kozyrev has instruments recording patterns of an unknown energy which is denser near the receiver and thinner near the sender of an action.[18] Dr. Ippolit Kogan reports "the moment of thought transmission is marked by drastic changes in the EEG tapes of both sender and receiver."[19] The Delawarr[20] and Kirlian[21] types of photography give evidence of a bioluminescence not visible to normal vision. Robert Pavlita's psychotronic generator gathers a bio-energy and converts it to definite uses.[22] Many scientists are exploring various bio-energies and are trying to find relationships and the general laws governing them. The many subtle cosmic fluctuations traversing space affect all living plants and animals. Measurable gravitational and electromagnetic influences penetrate everywhere in space.[23] F.A. Brown, Jr. has shown that the thick walls of a laboratory can control light and heat but do not shield a potato or oyster or chicken egg from cosmic forces. The positions of the sun, moon, and planets continually change the earth's magnetic field. Subtle changes in intensity of the geomagnetic field alter the electromagnetic field of plants, animals, and the nervous system of man. There are no uniform conditions on the earth since everything is influenced by cosmic forces; all are related.

We also need radical changes in our public education. Such changes need not limit the wealth of knowledge and technology achieved, need not even change the subject matter or structure of our organizations and curriculum. The significant change needed pertains to relationships between invisible energies and outer forms, the process or motion within the structure. The aliveness which transcends the form and which precedes the structure should be recognized in each activity or event, whether simple or complex. Man's responsibility should be to so order each act that he harmonizes and coordinates energies within himself before he releases them into action or outer expression.

Man has now reached a level of achievement that calls for self-direction, self-harmonizing of every thought and feeling projected; a conscious reorganization of self in relation to each expression; a conscious recognition that only action based upon inner and outer harmony is truly satisfying. Education ought to be based upon the process of thinking, the process of feeling, the process of releasing invisible energies consciously and later habitually, in relation to each functioning.

The mode of functioning which gives a balance between subtle energies releasing upward as the physical body rests downward gives a condition of freedom, openness, and inclusiveness. This foundation of existence should be renewed with each breath. Each thought and action springs from this primary foundation. The practice of yoga is based upon directing pranic currents to attain union with God, universal values, or one's Higher Self. But perhaps the time has come when instead of setting time apart for disciplines of union, we need to use ourselves as part of the oneness with each daily thought and act. Right thinking and right functioning produce right results.

Today most education focuses upon outward achievement in mental, emotional, and physical areas. A revolutionary focus upon the inner quality of organization would yield results far superior to those now achieved in areas of learning and expressing. The pupil should know intuitively when he feels ready for adequate action. Most pupils are not consciously aware that an internal organization, which they can direct, precedes action. They have neither been trained in sensitive awareness to the quality of organization nor in responsibility for self-direction.

Even a small child can feel the comfortable difference between a condition of balance in which subtle (pranic) energies release upward as the physical body rests downward. This can quickly become his primary habit of existence. Even a small child can experience the difference between a concise, well-defined goal or thought form and one which is not definite. A young child can quickly get the normal habit of releasing his lung breath and with it his energy breath (prana) just before he starts action or expression. He does not need to be aware that specific leverages within him automatically adjust then in relation to his entire concept of action. But very soon he learns to wait for a feeling of readiness before he moves into action. Sensitivity to the harmony within his being, uniting him with his concept and his goal, soon becomes his intuitive signal before he moves.

The intellectual approach to improve our educational system by interdisciplinary studies and integrative principles is good but misses the mark unless it is grounded on how the individual organism functions, and unless it gives directional knowledge and experience in the process of expression and action. Reorganizing just the knowledge or the courses of study can never yield integrative education, for it omits controlled adaptation of the individual unit. Each man must know himself; he must use and direct the capacities and forces within himself. Education should turn itself about and emphasize the process, the direction, and the way of thinking, feeling, and acting, rather than the end product. The integration must first be in man himself, in his flexible adjustment to each fact, object, person, thought, feeling, act, and force.

Ideation may be projected from a foundation of impersonal openness which is resilient yet inwardly calm with the correct use of energy breath or pranic currents. This is an essential base for adjusting to every intricate relationship in each act or expression. This is an essential conditioning foundation for all converging inclusiveness such as brotherhood, love, oneness, and knowledge of the Higher Self. Education of the future should be concerned with the process which takes place between an idea and its overt expression. The invariance in the process will be known in each of the transformations which take place whether in walking, inventing, meditating, listening, socializing, or resting.

The considerable work done with both children and adults has been most rewarding in developing these habits of a unitive, intuitive response and sensitivity. A start has revealed the critical nature of the timing of releases and "energy-balances" relative to leverages for specific action and specific psychological qualities. Martha S. Russell has charted the invariant pattern of these "energy-balances." A structure of sequence is indicated similar in every form of expression and action. This type of education calls for a whole new set of values focused on the nonmaterial energies available to man's use and direction. Authority from without is outmoded, and only self-direction is adequate.

Educators need an open-mindedness to perceive familiar problems in a new context as a relational pattern. We need teachers sensitive to the intuitive quiet mind, to the "transliminal state,"[24] to subtle energy factors such as motion within forms. But strangely (yet indicating we have not yet made the transition into the newer way of thinking) most teachers would prefer to hear that youths' interest in ecology, or their spiritual searching, or their psychism, or their scientific interests give hope for the future. Why are we so blind that we do not recognize that young people are suffocated by outer authority; that they have reached that state of development where self-directed activity is imperative? Our schools give little practice in self-direction or in awareness of organization of self in relation to thought, feeling, and action. Pupils are not sensitively aware of the process and the way they function. They have not been taught to discern the direction of thought and feeling. The newer forms of education will meet the challenge and will develop capacities of sensitivity, intuition, receptivity, creativity, and self-directed oneness.

Hopefully, scientists will soon more adequately explore and name the bio-energies used and will define what happens when ideational energies are released to focal points of balance for specific action. The individual should become more sensitive to the intuitional split-second timing releases (in relation to inner balances) that precede overt action. Oneness, unity, harmony, at every level of physical, emotional, mental, and spiritual functioning becomes daily experience as man achieves higher levels of mastery. Cooperation with universal order in using our physical and subtler equipment is our challenge now and in the future.

Society is in disorder because it has not been concerned with the essential transformations in the mind. When man has developed control of his mind so it may be indrawn from all external objects at will, when he has learned to control body, emotions, and mind in a serene calmness, he may perceive the radiance of his Higher Self and harmonize with it.

This Self, so subtle it cannot be described with words, or seen by ordinary vision, or fully comprehended by our physical senses, has been poetically described as dwelling in the heart of each being. This Self may be known only by a purified vision beyond physical limitations. We need awareness of the boundless imperishable power which dwells in the perishable body.

We need to be concerned with the artist rather than with his painting or any objects of knowledge or experience outside the artist. We need to study the radiation of consciousness. This energy which extends in space-time forms the field of consciousness we call life. It divides into lines of force, into forms and patterns. The energy of spirit is stepped down into the field of matter. N.Sri Ram points out that spiritual evolution is an "outflow of the energy from within" manifesting in a motion naturally, spontaneously, and free. In the life process this spiritual unfoldment is selfless without possessing or directing. It takes place when nature is purified.

All states of consciousness–waking, dreaming, sleeping, and all sense perceptions–are possible because the Self exists; the Higher Self is the reality by which man hears, sees, speaks. The visible and invisible are one; cause and effect are likewise two aspects of one force. The universe is evolved from the one force in various states of equilibrium between the incoming and outgoing energies.

Receptivity and the longing for consciousness of the Higher Self and God gradually adjust alignments within. Purified super-sensible awareness is attained when the body, emotions, and mind are in harmony; then all outgoing forces are controlled and incoming forces are received with complete openness and discrimination. To this end the potential available in man is gradually evolved and directed as the self merges with the Higher Self and the one Power.

REFERENCES

[1] Arthur W. Osborn, *The Expansion of Awareness* (Madras, India: The Theosophical Publishing House, 1961) p. 62.

[2] Annie Besant, *Esoteric Christianity* (Madras, India: The Theosophical Publishing House, 1946) p. 248.

[3] C. W. Leadbeater, *The Masters and the Path* (Wheaton, Illinois: The Theosophical Press, 1945).

[4] Mark 4:2.

[5] Matt. 7:6.

[6] Geoffrey Hodson, *The Hidden Wisdom in the Holy Bible* (Madras, India: The Theosophical Publishing House, 1963) p. 24.

[7] John 6:12.

[8] John 10:30.

[9] Col. 1:27.

[10] Eph. 4:6.

[11] F. L. Kunz, "The Reality of the Non-Material," *Main Currents in Modern Thought,* 20:34, Dec. 1963.

[12] Lawrence Le Shan, "Human Survival of Biological Death," *Main Currents in Modern Thought,* 26:35-36, Nov. Dec., 1969.

[13] *Ibid.,* pp. 40-43.

[14] J. Krishnamurti, *Commentaries on Living* (New York, N.Y.: Harper and Brothers Publishing Co., 1956) p. 73.

[15] *Ibid.,* pp. 73-74.

[16] Brian G. Cooper, "Religion and Technology Toward Dialogue," *Main Currents in Modern Thought,* 26; No. 1 Sept.-Oct., 1969, p. 11.

[17] Lancelot Law Whyte, "Recovery Values in a New Synthesis," *Main Currents in Modern Thought,* 26: Oct. 1969, pp. 6-7.

[18] Nikolai Kozyrev, "Possibility of Experimental Study of Properties of Time," *Joint Publication Research Service,* Dept. of Commerce, U.S.A. JPRS, No. 45238, May 1968.

[19] Shiela Ostrander and Lynn Schroeder, *Psychic Discoveries Behind the Iron Curtain,* (Englewood Cliffs, N.J.: Prentice Hall Inc. 1970) p. 21.

[20] George Delawarr and Douglas Baker, *Biomagnetism* (Oxford: Delawarr Laboratories Ltd. 1967).

[21] Ostrander and Schroeder, *op. cit.,* p. 196.

[22] *Ibid.,* p. 352.

[23] Michel Gauquelin, *The Cosmic Clocks* (Henry Regnery Co., 1967) p. 144.

[24] Harold Rugg, *Imagination* (New York, N.Y.: Harper & Row, 1963) p. 43.